Au présent du monde

Poèmes 2000–2009

AMINA SAÏD

Choix de poèmes et traduction de
Marilyn Hacker

The Present Tense
of the World

Poems 2000–2009

AMINA SAÏD

Translated by Marilyn Hacker

Black Widow Press is an imprint of Commonwealth Books, Inc., Boston, MA. Distributed to the trade by NBN (National Book Network) throughout North America, Canada, and the U.K. All Black Widow Press books are printed on acid-free paper, and glued into bindings. Black Widow Press and its logo are registered trademarks of Commonwealth Books, Inc.

Joseph S. Phillips and Susan J. Wood, Ph.D, Publishers
www.blackwidowpress.com

Cover Art and Page 18: Ahmed Ben Dhiab
Cover Design: Kerrie Kemperman
Text Design: Kerrie Kemperman

ISBN-13: 978-0-9842640-7-0

Printed in the United States

10 9 8 7 6 5 4 3 2 1

From
De décembre à la mer, 2001
La Douleur des seuils, 2002
Au présent du monde, 2006
L'Absence l'inachevé, 2009

All published by Les Éditions de la Différence, Paris, France

Some of these poems have appeared in *Banipal, Cerise Press, Cimarron Review, Field, The Manhattan Review, Mantis, Modern Poetry in Translation, New Letters, Poetry Daily, Prairie Schooner, Rattapallax, Wasafiri,* and *WordsWithoutBorders.*

"Freedom's Faces" appeared in *The Yale Anthology of 20th Century French Poetry*, Mary Ann Caws, Ed., Yale University Press, 2004.

"on the seventh day of my birth" appeared in *New European Poets*, Wayne Miller and Kevin Prufer, Eds., Graywolf Press, 2008.

Table

Table of Contents

AU PRÉSENT DU MONDE

L'ABSENCE L'INACHEVÉ

Introduction

If there existed a special/fortunate place of which we were continually in search—"exile" (we can thus name the state felt and experienced by many) would not only be geographical but metaphysical, what the poet Kathleen Raine calls "the errant spirit." An imaginary, utopian place, unlikely and ideal, that poetry can, for an instant's duration, let us glimpse. A symbolic place, never defined, where one would find oneself at last and attain unity. Perhaps everyone carries that "place" within. ("My body is my country," Adonis said in an interview). Perhaps it is in a symbol, a sign. "The sign has become the place," wrote Yves Bonnefoy.

—Amina Saïd, Le Maghreb littéraire, Vol III #5

Amina Saïd was born in Tunis in 1953 to a Tunisian father and a French mother during the struggle for Tunisian independence, which was achieved when she was three years old. She was thus raised bilingual, schooled both in literary Arabic and in French, with the dialectal Arabic of her country of birth also part of her life and linguistic imagination. As critic Inès Moatamri has noted, because of that parental configuration, French was literally her mother tongue, though the linguistic surround of her childhood was Arabophone. But the maternal figure was doubled by the presence of her Tunisian grandmother, Arabic-speaking, a "traditional" matriarch, mother of eight, who also passed those traditions on: a figure who reappears as a familial avatar in Saïd's poems, presaging her departure and celebrating her periodic returns.

> my grandmother appeared
> it's a sign she said you'll leave us soon
>
> ...

> *spilled green water on my footsteps*
> *so that you will return one day she said*
> *I was already on the other shore*
> ("Births", *La Douleur des seuils*)

The young girl was an omnivorous reader, of novels, biography, history. But Saïd's specific engagement with poetry came as much from the encouragement to write of a teacher of French in middle school, a poet herself, as from poetry-focused reading, though poetry in oral manifestation was around her in many forms:

> *child of the sun and the earth*
> *I recite the sacred verses*
> *the only girl among the boys*
> *sitting on the woven mat of the Coranic school*
> ("child of the sun and the earth",
> *Au présent du monde*)

At sixteen, Saïd went to Paris with her family (her father, who worked for UNESCO, was posted there), completed her baccalaureat, and entered university, in an environment that felt, she recalls, entirely foreign to her: not the language, but the landscape, and the light, or rather, its absence. Saïd studied English language and literature at university in Paris, a choice that, she has said, alleviated the difficulty of having to choose between her two native tongues. The deepening of her contact with English also brought an enthusiasm for the poetry of the British Romantics, Shelley and Keats in particular, and for that American romantic, Walt Whitman, whose work was a revelation to her. She later taught English for two years at university level in Tunisia, and has since translated several novels and short stories of the Filipino writer Francisco Sionil José from English into French, but it is clear that her literary imagination draws primarily from French and Arabic sources, and from a Mediterranean landscape. She has been living in Paris, despite the gray skies, since her mid-twenties, earning her living as a journalist, with frequent visits to the country of her birth.

Her work is part of a rich and growing Francophone Maghrebin literature in poetry, fiction and theater, whose modern and contemporary creators include Kateb Yacine, Mohammed Dib, Mohammed Khair-Eddine, Assia Djebbar, Leïla Sebbar, Habib Tengour, Rachida Madani and Tahar Bekri: all of them writers born in the Maghreb, bilingual or even more polyglot, who chose French as their language of literary expression. And, I might add, the not always separate Middle Eastern Francophone poetic tradition represented today by poets like Vénus Khoury-Ghata and Salah Stétié.

What does it mean for a writer whose culture and upbringing are those of a formerly colonized people still suffering from or coping with the aftereffects of colonization to write in the (former) "master's language." And what are the complications added when the "master's language" is at the same time the literal mother tongue? It is notable that many of the writers who are children of North African/French marriages have made this choice: Leïla Sebbar, Nina Bouraoui, Hédi Kaddour. Still, the exemplar would be the entirely Maghrebin (Algerian) playwright, poet, and novelist Kateb Yacine, who would not have hesitated to proclaim, like the speaker of Mahmoud Darwish's "Identity Card," "Write down — I am an Arab," and who *did* write (in 1966): "Francophony is a neocolonial political machine, which only perpetuates our alienation, but the usage of the French language does not mean that one is an agent of a foreign power, and I write in French to tell the French that I am not French." He was (nonetheless?) awarded the French government's Grand Prix national des lettres in 1987.

Kateb Yacine's work was championed by Sartre, by French avant-garde publishers, and theater directors (even while his first play was banned in France during the Algerian war of independence). The contemporary Maghrebin writer living in France is also a French writer, and North African-rooted fiction writers and scenarists have provided some of the richest and most innovative contemporary work, just as French artists of North African origin have revitalized popular music. For poets, though, there is the peculiarly French problem of the largely prevalent refusal of historical, ethnic, or regional particularity in poetry—excepting the particularity of the individual consciousness. In this context, even a lyrical *"retour au pays natal"* is iconoclastic (in a parallel register to something like Franck Venaille's working-class Paris), and sets the poet enough apart from a certain mainstream modernity that she might as well be writing in her "other language/with its hidden vowels".

Who, then, are the readers of Francophone Maghrebin writers' poetry? For their fiction, the answer would be "most readers." But everyone who reads fiction doesn't read poetry, and in France (even more than in the United States) those who do are often self-enclosed in literary schools and the pursuit of post-modernity. Often, these poets, and Francophone poets from the Mashreq, have a wider readership amongst the French-speaking populations of North Africa and the Middle East, and the rest of the French-speaking world (in Canada, Guadeloupe, Martinique, La Réunion), and a receptive public, often reached through international poetry festivals, among readers of French in other European and Latin American countries (including a significant population of the Arab diaspora).

Since her first collection in 1980, Saïd has published fourteen books of poems, all in France or as co-editions with a Québecois publisher. In the 1990s, Saïd also published two volumes of re-invented Tunisian folk-tales. There is something of the re-invented folk-tale in many of her poems as well, tales of origin as in "child of the sun and the earth," the personification of the elements in "Freedom's Faces," or an elaboration of the Seven Sleepers legend common to Muslims and Eastern Christians in "Like the axe forgotten at the foot of the tree." But just as folk-tale may well have strong links with ritual, history and religious or spiritual practice, the narrative clarity of some of Saïd's poems at once masks and opens the way to a more complex cosmogony.

More than for many contemporary poets, there is a characteristic vocabulary associated with her work, like an underlying sketch: the sky and its silence, the sea in its permutations, natural light, the human eye, stone, exile: an impossible eternal return to a landscape of childhood. The apprenticeship of letters, with the image of calligraphy there attached (whether or not, in fact, the first language she learned to write was Arabic), and an age, seven, marking the initiation, is a key moment, a "volta," in several poems:

> seven years old I swam in black waters
> on the light-path traced by the moon
> as far as the sun's dead end
> as far as the land of limits
> I took mirage lessons
> scribe outside time
> inscribing centuries in calligraphy
> with the sea's blue ink
> > ("Births", La Douleur des seuils)

> in the seventh year of my birth
> I dreamed what had been
> on the world's lined page
> I traced letter after letter
> to remind myself
> of what I had to forget
> and of what in me was already dying
> > ("on the seventh day of my birth",
> > Au présent du monde)

The change that absence has wrought on her, and the implicit irony of having become an "Occidental" to Maghrebin eyes, as well as that perpetual other, an artist, does not escape the writer:

> beneath the poet's portrait
> the child from Hadj-Diddeh asks me
> did you know Rimbaud, ma'am?
> ("Blood of the Sea", De décembre à la mer)

Amina Saïd has also traveled widely, in part to present her work at innumerable international festivals: the idea of certain human verities, not all of them pleasant, that remain constant though the scenery and language change is also her preoccupation, as well as the more optimistic possibility of dialogue among the speakers of many languages, the mutual comprehension of widely different fields of experience and reference. Both the "eternal return" to the *pays natal*, to scenes of childhood in another language and to a constantly rewritten myth of origin and emergence, and the theme of travel and encounter with the multiple stranger who is often nonetheless a brother/sister figure, are consistent with the idea of *"errance"* in Saïd's poems, a word difficult to render in English, as it is not strictly a journey, still less "wandering", which seems to have no aim, and not a pilgrimage either. The Tunisian critic and poet Najeh Jegham suggested as an equivalent for Saïd's *"errance"* the Arabic *siyâha*, which meant, in the writings of Ibn Arabi, the gnostic's journey of exploration for the purpose of learning—a word which, alas, in contemporary parlance, is used to mean "tourism".

In this context, the relative absence of France (and of Paris, her long-time home) in Saïd's work, at least in the books published in this decade, is notable—while, along with the actual and imagined returns to Tunisia depicted, there are views of Durban, Medellín, Amsterdam, Manila, Gorée, sites of colonial but also European history. When a homeless man in the Gare de Lyon becomes the speaker of a poem, it is like a light illuminating a radically different setting: the man himself is a displaced Maghrebin who begins to resemble a Sufi beggar-pilgrim in his self-portrayal, and in his claim of identity with the posited listener. The relationship of temporal travel, so much a part of this poet's experience, with spiritual travel, is not unexamined in Saïd's work, as she noted, again in *Le Maghreb littéraire*:

> *Poetry is movement, spiritual journey: the real journey is interior, an ontological as well as a topographical quest. ("Ontology is coming to understand the verb 'to be'" according to Lévinas). And from there the idea of a progression, of a rite of passage, of continual renewal—"hoping to be able, oneself, to*

15

*re-make oneself", (Valéry), the "perfecting of the soul" without which there is no perfecting of the poem's words (Ungaretti). We create in recreating ourselves, are born through the poem created, which creates us in turn, makes us **be**, knowing all the while that we must continually "move beyond" (Hugo). Poetry thus allows or facilitates the transformation of experience into spiritual knowledge, the arrival at a certain degree of consciousness and "the consciousness of the self is at the same time the consciousness of everything" (Lévinas), and thus of what exists, lives, on earth.*

Though Saïd's poems are most often spoken in the first person singular, it is misleading to unfailingly associate that 'I' with the poet, and not only in poems like those dealing with the Seven Sleepers, or spoken by the homeless man. Sometimes an epigraph indicates that a poem is, if not precisely a dramatic monologue, possessed of a double consciousness, like the complex "Path of Light", which opens with a quote from the Sufi mystic and poet Rabi'a al-'Adawiyya. The poem can be read at once as the description of an interior ordeal, both erotic and spiritual, and as a narrative not recounting but representing Rabi'a's life and quest. Even the "return" poems are as much about an idea of childhood, the acquisition of knowledge and the loss of an Edenic landscape as they are autobiographical. If anything, the poet reveals more of "herself" in the poems about the other sort of travel, outward, to South Africa, Chile, the Netherlands or the Philippines, where the speaking consciousness, that of an observer, is hungry for history, scenery, tastes, smells, sounds, exchanges of speech. There is a different kind of revelation in the selection from the last section of *L'Absence l'inachevé* (2009) which is a prolonged elegy for the poet's father, whose (beloved) presence was the strongest link to the home country and to its language always echoing in the poet's French. But here too, the sequence's condensed and piercing grief rises to an orchestral and mythical pitch with the long stanzaic final poem, its tragic chorus of bereaved "mothers" foreseeing perpetual loss calling to mind both Euripides' "The Trojan Women" and the mourning of doomed Zainab in Shi'a Muslim ritual—larger and more measured than any individual grief.

After *L'Absence l'inachevé*, Amina Saïd has turned toward a more expansive poetry, still in progress, which is prefigured in some of the work here. She is writing a narrative trilogy comprising an expanded work in dramatic monologues on the theme of the Seven Sleepers, a long poem on a 14th-century maritime voyage by an Arab explorer, including tales-within-tales recited by the ship's storyteller, and a final narrative poem on the exploits of Dhul Qarnayn, a mythical ruler sometimes identified with Alexander the Great (or Iskander in Arabic). Her choice of narratives, besides, of course, the poet's pleasure in discovering a new source from which language will spring, was influenced by the desire to retell stories common to the Muslim and Judaeo-Christian/Oriental and Occidental traditions, a desire at once profoundly contemporary and growing directly from the centuries-long Mediterranean marriage of cultures from which she springs.

De décembre à la mer

JE ME PRÉSENTE AU MONDE

En poésie, on n'habite que le lieu que l'on quitte.
~René Char

Le poème qui suit fut composé au cours d'un séjour au pays natal en juillet, le mois de ma naissance, c'est pourquoi «ici» dans le texte se réfère à «là-bas».

je me présente au monde
à mes ombres mêlée
un cri suffit pour saluer la terre
le ciel et mon visage à venir

ici le soleil est de feu brûlant
je me présente au monde
qui depuis toujours oscille
au rythme des jours et des nuits

ici des pins plantent leurs aiguilles
dans une argile rouge
l'eau reste parcimonieuse
j'ignore encore ce qu'apporte le vent

je me présente au monde
à la mer offre mon premier regard
un poisson une main ouverte
préservent les habitants des maisons

ici les vagues sont messagères
du cerne mauve de l'horizon
sur la rive frangée dansent
leurs calligraphies d'algues et d'écume

I INTRODUCE MYSELF TO THE WORLD

In poetry, you only live in the place you're leaving.
~René Char

The following poem was composed during a stay in Tunisia, the country of my birth, in July, my birth month: "here" in the text refers to "there."

I introduce myself to the world
mixed with my own shadows
a cry is enough to greet the earth
the sky and my forthcoming face

here the sun is made of burning fire
I introduce myself to the world
which has always swayed
in the rhythm of nights and days

here pines plant their needles
in red clay
water is frugal here
I still don't know what the wind will bring

I introduce myself to the world
offer the sea my first look
a fish an open hand
protect the houses' dwellers

here the waves are messengers
of the horizon's purple ring
their letters of algae and foam
dance on the fringed shore

mais les femmes du littoral
suivent des chemins de terre
personne jamais n'a voulu
apprivoiser le libre horizon

je me présente au monde
brillent par-dessus mon épaule
l'étoile neuve le croissant
demain encore le sirocco

une mèche noire colle à mon front
j'ai le regard des miens
l'aïeule l'a reconnu
dans le fond des grands miroirs

assise aux feux de leurs reflets
drapée de chatoyantes étoffes
elle convoquait ses morts
depuis sa tombe s'est perdue

ici les sourciers de l'oubli
ne trouvent plus de puits
des jardins entiers s'effacent
sous la langue ensablée des oiseaux

la terre est lourde d'humanité
êtres et choses qui la parent
sont oeuvres de l'ici et de cet ailleurs
que fixe le regard des morts

ici terre et pierre sont mémoire
les saints reposent dans une pénombre
propice aux enchantements
ici même les miracles sont discrets

but the women of the coast
follow earthen roads
no one has ever wished
to tame the free horizon

I introduce myself to the world
burning above my shoulder
the new star the crescent moon
sirocco again tomorrow

a black curl clings to my forehead
I look out at the world like my kin
the great-grandmother recognized it
deep in her tall mirrors

in their reflected fire
she sits draped in glimmering cloth
she has been convening her dead
since the site of her grave was lost

the diviners of oblivion
find no more sources here
whole gardens fade away
under the birds' silted tongue

the earth is heavy with humans
beings and things which bedeck it
are the works of here and that elsewhere
fixed in the stare of the dead

here earth and stone are remembrance
the saints rest in a half-light
propitious to magic spells
even miracles are discreet here

en ce lieu premier
les corps devancent leur ombre
à quels mystérieux continents
renvoie le songe des yeux clos

je me présente au monde
ici l'être se libère
en découvrant le fil
au creux du labyrinthe

ici règnent tous les temps
les visages s'ajustent aux visages
et la distance finit
par nous confondre avec nous-mêmes

le temps est une lagune comblée
une langue de terre resurgie des eaux
une montagne mythique éternelle et bleue
une colonne dressée face à la baie

ici meurent et renaissent les siècles
pour nourrir le désir des hommes
ils s'en vont pour mieux revenir
ici les absents n'ont jamais tort

car on ne part que contraint
ailleurs est ce miroir
où l'on quête une autre image
un chemin qui mène à sa propre histoire

ici la lumière est une mise à nu
il nous faut en retrouver la source
il nous faut décrypter le jour
incrusté de sel et de feu

in this primordial place
bodies outdistance their shadows
back to what strange continents
do closed eyes' reveries send me

I introduce myself to the world
here one sets oneself free
by discovering the thread
in the pit of the labyrinth

all ages rule here at once
faces fit onto faces
and distance finishes
by confusing us with ourselves

time is a filled-in lagoon
a tongue of earth re-emerged from the water
a mythic eternal blue mountain
a pillar raised facing the bay

here centuries die and are reborn
to nourish men's desires
they leave to return in strength
here the absent are never wrong

for you only leave under constraint
elsewhere is that mirror
where you beg for another image
a road that leads to your own story

here the light strips everything bare
we must rediscover its source
we must decode the day
incrusted with salt and fire

ici la lumière est vivant pilier
du ciel à la crête aveugle des pierres
elle supporte le lent
déroulement de la nuit

et comme chacun s'inquiète
du retour des ténèbres
éclate l'ardeur des chants
que pacifie la joie

ici le désert sculpte
un chant à sa mesure
que l'homme s'en va
cueillir de dune en dune

ici sont d'autres lois
dans la volière des mots
chacun choisit avec soin
celui qui l'émerveillera

ici chaque jour qui naît
rappelle au ciel ses serments
ici la terre a soif
de cette pluie d'étoiles

ici la réalité n'est visible
que pour l'oeil du coeur
l'invisible nous hante
de ses images contrariées

ici la nuit baignée de lune
s'accorde aux êtres
je tente d'en saisir le cercle
se dérobe son visage martelé

here the light is a living pillar
from the sky to the stones' blind ridges
it supports the slow
unwinding of the night

and since each one is uneasy
at the return of darkness
the heat of song bursts forth
which is calmed by joy

here the desert also sculpts
a song to its measure
which men go gathering
from dune to dune

here are other laws
in the aviary of words
each carefully chooses
an astonishing one

here each day as it's born
reminds the sky of its oaths
here the earth is thirsty
for that rain of stars

reality can be seen here
by the heart's eye only
the invisible haunts us
with its thwarted images

here the moon-bathed night
concurs with human life
I try to grasp its circle
its hammered face shies away

tombé dans le ventre de la citerne
il tremble sur la noire surface
puis se dissout
je ne peux boire de cette eau

un coq chante en plein minuit
au matin qui ne sait rien des adieux
s'éveillent ces terres d'indolence
du secret d'un long sommeil

citerne où tourbillonnent les esprits
dans le patio des légendes
deux tourterelles de sable
prennent soudain leur envol

falls in the cistern's belly
it trembles on the black surface
then dissolves
I cannot drink that water

a cock crows just at midnight
to a morning which knows no farewells
those languid lands awake
from a long sleep's secret

cistern where spirits swirl
from the courtyard of often-told tales
two turtledoves of sand
suddenly take flight

VISAGES DE LA LIBERTÉ

1.

je fus ténèbres
d'où naquirent ciel et terre
dit la nuit

dès lors ce qu'il est de céleste
sur la terre
rendit les êtres visibles
et prêts à suivre leur route

ce qu'il est de terrestre
dans le ciel
rendit les astres visibles
et prêts à suivre leur route

2.

j'ai toujours voyagé avec le ciel
et le silence qui le porte

il a pour double toutes mes eaux
dit la terre

elles lui sont mouvants miroirs
où il se crée mille surprises

aucun de ses visages
ne m'est étranger

FREEDOM'S FACES

1.

I was the darkness
from which heaven and earth were born
says the night

since then what is celestial
on earth
makes its creatures visible
and able to go their way

and what is terrestrial
in the sky
makes its stars visible
and able to go their way

2.

I have always traveled with the sky
and the silence which carries him

he is twinned by my waters
says the earth

they are his moving mirrors
in which he gives himself a thousand surprises

none of his faces
is strange to me

son souffle est caresse brisée
et face à face nous avons vécu
dans le présent du présent
et dans celui du passé

quand je n'étais que pierre et chaos
déjà j'existais dans son règne
et emplissais son vide

3.

je viens au jour
de la nuit nue

d'entre les courbes sacrées de la terre

je suis lien dit la source
entre deux mondes

j'abandonne ma bouche
au pur miroitement du ciel

je ne connais du voyage
que l'élan de pierre en pierre

le silence prend ma voix

à suivre les routes effacées du hasard
je sais la mesure de la solitude

celui qui se penche vers moi
donne son visage à ma liberté

his breath is a broken caress
and face to face we've lived
in the present of the present
and that of the past

when I was nothing but rocks and chaos
I already existed in his kingdom
and filled its emptiness

3.

I come to the day
from naked night

from between the earth's sacred curves

I am the link says the spring
between two worlds

I abandon my mouth
to the pure glimmering of the sky

I know no journey
but the leap from stone to stone

silence takes my voice

to follow overgrown trails of chance
I know the dimensions of solitude

anyone who bends over me
gives his face to my freedom

4.

je n'existe dit le vent
que par ma folie

le sable dans mes veines
est rouge preuve de vie

l'oiseau en mes courants
est mené par mon souffle

je loge en la plus haute tour
berce le fruit prolixe
de vos jours doux-amers

je ranime l'éternelle flamme
pousse les océans vers la terre
rien ne m'arrête

je suis le même en chaque lieu
sous d'autres noms on me révère

l'écho
naît de la vibration qu'il engendre
et moi colportant l'écho
sur le silence je prends
ma revanche

j'anime le cerf-volant des âmes
car l'âme vit
à tous les étages du monde

le temps du rêve est sa demeure
d'où elle sourit aux étoiles

4.

I only exist, says the wind
through my own madness

the sand in my veins
is the red proof of life

the bird in my airstreams
is led by my breath

I inhabit the highest tower
cradle the talkative fruit
of your bittersweet days

I rekindle the eternal flame
push the oceans towards the earth
nothing stops me

I am the same in every place
I am revered under other names

an echo
is born from the vibration it begets
and spreading the echo
on silence, I get
my revenge

I set souls' kites in motion
because the soul lives
on every floor of the world

dream-time is its dwelling
from where it smiles at the stars

qu'elle croit s'absenter
veille le fil tendu

5.

ma flamme est droite
dit le soleil hymne
au jour qui me soutient

je brosse les paysages du monde
lui donne les couleurs de mon feu

si je brûle le passé
je ne sais rien de l'avenir

mes cycles annoncent
les cataclysmes

coursier du mirage
que nulle flèche n'atteint
je m'élève et le ciel n'est plus

qu'embrasement de lumière
espace de ma liberté

6.

je suis le fleuve
au sourire transparent

mon éternelle errance
me sert de langage

it may think it's leaving
the taut string keeps watch

5.

My flame is erect
says the sun a hymn
to the day which upholds me

I brush on the world's landscapes
give them the colors of my fire

if I burn the past
I know nothing of the future

my cycles announce
cataclysms

steed of the mirage
that no arrow can touch
I arise and the sky is only

a blaze of light
space of my freedom

6.

I am the river
whose smile is transparent

my endless wandering
becomes my language

sans rien saisir
tout au long du voyage
vers le temps aveugle des mers
depuis toujours je glisse

de cette nuit sans fin
que nous nommons mystère
je peuple leurs abîmes

7.

je suis ferveur
j'improvise dit le feu

tantôt étincelle tantôt brasier
déchaînement furieux
je me dévore moi-même

je suis cette force qui tord le mors
et concentré dans son oeil fou
dompte le cheval le plus fort

quand les oiseaux de bronze
tiraient des flèches de leur corps
c'est dans mes flammes
qu'ils quêtaient les foudres du ciel

ici mangeur de morts
là peuplant l'enfer des hommes
je fonds les métaux les plus purs

si la fumée voile ma lumière
je provoque une autre lumière

taking hold of nothing
during the whole voyage
towards the seas' blind time
I slide forever

out of this endless night
which we call mystery
I populate their depths

7.

I am ardor
I improvise, says the fire

sometimes spark sometimes blaze
furious outburst
alone I devour myself

I am that force which twists the bit
and concentrated in his mad eyes
tames the mightiest horse

when bronze birds
plucked arrows from their bodies
it was in my flames
that they sought the sky's lightning-bolts

here devouring the dead
there peopling hell with humans
I melt the purest metals

if smoke veils my light
I spark another light

8.

je suis la barque présente
aux rives de la mort

voilée de limpides ténèbres
je transporte les âmes destinées
à l'espace doré d'un jour perpétuel

ombres auxquelles le destin
donnera peut-être un autre visage

8.

I am the skiff that's present
on the shores of death

veiled with limpid darkness
I transport destined souls
to the golden space of endless day

shades to which fate
will perhaps give other faces

de la mémoire de la mer
aux bonheurs de la terre
de février à mai
des rives de la nuit nue
aux rochers sombres du jour
de l'âme au corps
de l'accueil fait à la vie
à notre exigence sans fin
du vide à la présence
du sommeil à la veille
de l'absence au rêve
du proche au lointain
de la lune au soleil
des abords de l'ombre
aux bras de la lumière
de l'obscur à la transparence
de la vie à son contraire
de la pierre à l'étoile
de la racine à la branche
et de la cendre au feu
de la révolte pure
à la sagesse inquiète
de l'ailleurs à l'ici
d'une langue à l'autre
de l'effacement au visible
du visible à la transcendance
de la forme à une réalité autre
de la solitude au souvenir
du vivre à son angoisse
de l'horizon au poème
et du poème au silence
de l'origine à la fin
du temps passé à l'instant ailé

from the memory of the sea
to the bliss of the earth
from February to May
from the shores of bare night
to the dark rocks of day
from soul to body
from the welcome given life
to our endless demands
from emptiness to presence
from sleep to waking
from absence to dream
from near to far
from the moon to the sun
from the realms of shadow
to the arms of light
from darkness to clarity
from life to its opposite
from the stone to the star
from the root to the branch
and from ash to fire
from unalloyed revolt
to uneasy wisdom
from elsewhere to here
from one tongue to another
from erasure to visibility
from visibility to transcendence
from form to a different reality
from solitude to memory
from life to the dread of it
from the horizon to the poem
and from the poem to silence
from the source to the end
from past time to winged instant

de l'enfance à l'exil
et de l'exil à la fin de cet exil
du détour au retour
du masque au visage
de l'être à ses possibles
de l'audace au don
et du chant à la grâce
de l'espace du ciel
à celui du tombeau
de l'infime au tout
du relatif à l'absolu
de ce qui n'est pas à ce qui est
des signes du rêve
aux erreurs du matin
de la passion à l'amour
de l'oeil au rivage
des mots au destin
nous ne cessons d'errer
en quête d'un lieu
qui n'a pas de lieu

from childhood to exile
and from exile to exile's end
from detour to return
from the mask to the face
from what is to what might
from the dare to the gift
and from song to grace
from the span of the sky
to the space of the grave
from tiny to infinite
from relative to absolute
from what's not to what is
from the signs in a dream
to the morning's mistakes
from passion to love
from the eye to the shore
from words to fate
we roam unceasingly
in search of a place
for which there is no place

LE SANG DE LA MER

Si j'ai du goût, ce n'est guère
Que pour la terre et les pierres.
~Arthur Rimbaud

1.

Djibouti
étoile variable
sous l'arc chaviré de la lune

Djibouti
carrefour de poussière

des enfants nus jouent
au bord de la mer Rouge

berger du temps l'homme
regarde vers l'éternité du désert

nous sommes les pèlerins de l'errance
dit le poète

2.

réseau secret des pistes

ombre des pierres en prière
cercle sacré
pour les saints en palabre
pierres sur pierres
pierres pour la vie
pierres pour la mort

BLOOD OF THE SEA

If I hunger, it's only
For earth and for stones.
~Rimbaud

1.

Djibouti
unstable star
beneath the moon's capsized arc

Djibouti
crossroads of dust

naked children play
on the shore of the Red Sea

time's shepherd man
looks towards the desert's eternity

we are the pilgrims of errancy
says the poet

2.

secret network of trails

shadow of stones at prayer
sacred circle
for chattering saints
stones upon stones
stones for life
stones for death

3.

sur les enfants de Dammerjog
veillent les ancêtres
une chèvre médite dans la cour
l'oiseau tisse son nid sur l'arbre du ciel

4.

qu'es-tu venue faire dans mon pays
dit le conte de l'écolier de Boulaos
et que cherches-tu?

5.

Maskali
bateau blanc
à la rencontre d'un rêve d'île
arc-boutée sur la passion de la mer
où suis-je s'il n'y a que l'horizon?

nous abordons l'anse de sable
ici les arbres sont de corail

6.

canyon gouffre peuplé de djinns
comme en écho à la nuit
de mes cauchemars d'enfant

7.

Goubet al-Kharâb cônes de désolation
seins jumeaux
que baigna le sang de la mer

3.

the ancestors watch over
the children of Dammerjog
a goat meditates in the courtyard
the bird weaves its nest on the tree of sky

4.

what have you come to do in my country
says the tale of the schoolboy from Boulaous
and what are you looking for?

5.

Maskali
white boat
come to meet an island dream
buttressed on the sea's passion
where am I if there's nothing but horizon-line?

we approach the sandy cove
the trees here are made of coral

6.

canyon chasm inhabited by djinns
echoing the dark
of my childhood nightmares

7.

Goubet el-Kharâb cones of desolation
twin breasts
bathed by the sea's blood

8.

pierres sur pierres
pierres noircies par tous les péchés du monde

pierres dispersées sur le feu de la terre
perles d'ambre gris du chapelet divin

pierres à main droite
pierres à main gauche
pierres pour la vie
pierres pour la mort
l'enfer le paradis n'ont pas de frontières

9.

chameaux chèvres gazelles
tel un signe au-dessus de nous
un rapace franchit l'espace

quelques arbres implorent le blanc des nuages
buée de larmes
autant de prières parties en fumée

10.

entaille coutelade balafre
dans la chair minérale
béance de la faille
échappée vers le néant

11.

oeil grand ouvert sous le suaire de sel
le lac Assal fixe le soleil à son zénith

8.

stones upon stones
stones darkened by all the world's sins

stones scattered on the earth's fire
ambergris pearls of the holy rosary

stones to the right
stones to the left
stones for life
stones for death
hell and heaven have no borders

9.

camels goats gazelles
like a sign above us
a hawk breaches space

a few trees implore the clouds' whiteness
a condensation of tears
as many prayers gone up in smoke

10.

gash, knife-wound, scar
in the mineral flesh
yawning gap in the fault
view of the abyss

11.

wide-open eye beneath a shroud of salt
Lake Assal pins the sun at zenith

cristaux de pure lumière
caravanes pétrifiées dans le temps du monde

salure eaux d'amertume brûlante
eaux vierges veines liquides

qui frappa la pierre
pour que jaillisse la source?

12.

pierres brutes pierres libres
pions ocres et noirs sur l'échiquier géant
chicots du rire édenté de la terre
bornes de Satan
il n'y a pas de pierre heureuse

13.

mémoire barbelée
étreignant un sol d'airain

ligne de démarcation
rempart d'épines dont se joue le vent

les nomades sont entrés dans la ville

14.

sous le portrait du poète
l'enfant de Hadj-Diddeh me demande
madame as-tu connu Rimbaud?

crystals of pure light
caravans petrified as the world ages

saline waters of burning bitterness
virgin waters liquid veins

who struck the stone
so that the source gushed forth?

12.

brute stones free stones
black and ochre pawns on the giant chessboard
stumps in the earth's toothless laughter
Satan's landmarks
there are no happy stones

13.

barbed memory
gripping the bronze soil

line of demarcation
rampart of thorns played with by the wind

the nomads have entered the city

14.

beneath the poet's portrait
the child from Hadj-Diddeh asks me
did you know Rimbaud, ma'am?

COMME LA HACHE AU PIED DE L'ARBRE OUBLIÉE

> *C'est que les spectres ne dorment pas*
> *Nos rêves sont leur nourriture préférée.*
> —Heiner Müller

En l'an 250, à Éphèse, en Turquie, sous le règne de l'empereur romain Dèce, les chrétiens furent persécutés. Sept jeunes hommes trouvèrent refuge dans une caverne, où ils furent emmurés vivants. Une légende naquit, celle des Sept Dormants, selon laquelle ils se réveillèrent d'un sommeil de trois siècles, et témoignèrent de leur persécution et de leur attente de la résurrection. Dans le Coran, cette tradition est reprise dans la sourate «La Caverne». Il y est dit que «les gens de la caverne» étaient accompagnés d'un chien. Sans doute en raison de l'importance du dogme de la résurrection et du culte des saints communs aux religions chrétienne et musulmane, cette tradition a fait le tour de la Méditerranée, et on la retrouve tant au Maghreb qu'en Bretagne et jusqu'en Indonésie.

comme la hache au pied de l'arbre oubliée
nous avons dormi plusieurs siècles
tous les sept dépouillés de nos ornements
de ténèbres et revêtus de lumière

nous sommes nés nous sommes morts
nous allons renaître
quitter l'ombre tiède de la caverne
gardienne du miracle de notre exil

oubliés des hommes et des étoiles
enveloppés dans le suaire du sommeil
mais soumis à l'attrait de l'horizon
nous avons respiré notre propre poussière
notre langue avait goût de cendres

LIKE THE AXE FORGOTTEN AT THE FOOT OF THE TREE

> *For phantoms don't sleep*
> *Our dreams are their favorite food.*
> —Heiner Müller

In the year 250 AD, in Ephesus, in Turkey, under the reign of the Roman emperor Decius, the Christians were persecuted. Seven young men took shelter in a cave, where they were walled up alive. A legend was born, that of the Seven Sleepers, according to which they awoke from three centuries of sleep, and bore witness to their persecution and to their expectation of resurrection. In the Koran, this legend is recounted in the sourat known as "the Cave." It is written there that "the people of the cave" were accompanied by a dog. Doubtless because the dogma of resurrection and the cult of saints is common and important to both the Christian and Muslim religions, this legend made its way around the Mediterranean; one finds it in North Africa, in Brittany and as far away as Indonesia.

like the axe forgotten at the foot of the tree
we have slept for centuries
all seven of us stripped of our vestments
of darkness and arrayed with light

we were born we died
we will be reborn
and leave the cave's warm darkness
that watched over our exile's miracle

forgotten by men and stars
folded in sleep's shroud
but subject to the horizon's attraction
we breathed our own dust
our speech had a taste of ash

nous étions des hommes qui rêvent

nous avons rêvé du jour rayonnant
dans la procession des nuits

nous avons rêvé d'étoiles souterraines
de roses de pierre entrelacées
de rivières blanches et de lunes fiévreuses
d'astres innocents en leur mort première

nous avons rêvé de mirages et d'îles
d'intarissables sources de femmes douces
d'arbres d'oiseaux prêts à l'envol
de démons d'anges d'éternité heureuse

dans le sillage du soleil nos corps
glissaient sur une barque de silence

nous avons fait rêves d'hommes

en rêve nous avons vu s'ouvrir
et se refermer les ailes de la grande nuit
paupières géantes sur l'oeil de l'univers

dans nos corps cette nuit étanchait
sa soif de sel et de sang

en rêve nous avons vu la terre entamée
d'autres oiseaux tournoyer dans le ciel intérieur
un portail clos donnant sur le tombeau

comme la hache au pied de l'arbre oubliée
nous avons connu une nuit longue comme la mort
mais ce n'était pas la mort

we were men who dreamed

we have dreamed of radiant day
in the procession of nights

we have dreamed of underground comets
of entwined rock roses
of white streams and feverish moons
of innocent stars in their first death

we have dreamed of mirages and islands
of inexhaustible springs and gentle women
of trees where birds prepare to take flight
of demons angels and glad eternity

in the sun's wake our bodies
drifted on a skiff of silence

our dreams were men's dreams

in our dream we saw the wings
of the great night open and close
giant lids on the eyes of the universe

in our bodies night quenched
its thirst for salt and blood

in our dream we saw earth exhausted
other birds circling the inner sky
a closed gateway leading to the grave

like the axe forgotten at the foot of the tree
we knew a night as long as death
but it was not death

nous avions franchi les portes d'une autre vie
ce n'était pas le temps qui passait
nous étions hors du temps

ainsi avons-nous dormi plusieurs siècles
à nos côtés une image de chien fidèle

un souvenir de lieu occupait notre veille
cent fois nous l'avons fui sommes revenus
repartis jamais n'avons songé aux adieux

tous les sept en notre refuge
étions comme graines repliées
dans leur sommeil terrestre
en attente de lumière et d'eau

nous étions à l'aube d'un commencement

nous sommes nés nous sommes morts
nous allons renaître
reprendre les sentiers solaires
qui conduisent à la vie
cueillir les fruits lourds de notre exil

vacillants déjà nous nous dressons
au bord de la lumière
à nos côtés l'ombre de notre ombre
cette éphémère compagne

bercés par toutes les naissances
et toutes les morts passées et à venir
nous avons à la fois l'âge
de notre naissance celui de notre mort

we crossed the threshold of another life
what passed was not time
we were outside time

and we slept like that for centuries
at our side the image of a faithful dog

the memory of a place filled our vigil
a hundred times we fled it we returned
left once more never thought of farewells

all seven of us in our refuge
were like seeds folded
in their earthy sleep
waiting for light and water

we were at the dawn of a beginning

we were born we died
we will be reborn
set forth again on solar roads
which lead to life
gather the ripe fruits of our exile

wavering already we rise
at the light's edge
at our sides the shadow of our shadow
that transient companion

rocked by all the births
and deaths past and to come
we are at once as old as
we were at our birth and at our death

La Douleur des seuils

NAISSANCES

je suis née sur les bords
de la mer du soleil couchant
la grande mer la très verte
la mer des Philistins
celle qui baigna Carthage
la mer blanche intérieure des Arabes
dont les chevaux déferlèrent sur les rives

*

algue j'ai grandi vague poisson
étoile aux multiples branches
la première lettre de l'alphabet
incrustée sur le front

*

à sept ans je nageais sur les eaux noires
dans le chemin de lumière que traçait la lune
j'allais jusqu'à l'impasse du soleil
jusqu'au pays des limites
je prenais des leçons de mirage
scribe intemporel
appliqué à calligraphier les siècles
à l'encre bleue de la mer

BIRTHS

I was born on the shore
of the sea of the setting sun
the great sea the greenest
the sea of the Philistines
in which Carthage was bathed
the white inland sea of the Arabs
whose horses stream onto its banks

                    *

like seaweed I grew a wave a fish
a many-branched star
the first letter of the alphabet
inlaid on my forehead

                    *

seven years old I swam in black waters
on the light-path traced by the moon
as far as the sun's dead end
as far as the land of limits
I took mirage lessons
scribe outside time
inscribing centuries in calligraphy
with the sea's blue ink

*

à neuf ans je découvris éblouie une ville engloutie
au retour je mis mes ailes à sécher sur les dunes
je comptais les pierres avant de les ramasser
j'avais deux visages je vivais dans deux mondes

*

à onze ans je ne parlais déjà plus à personne
pourtant une langue naissait dans ma bouche
je cherchais dans le silence les secrets du poème
essayais de me définir dans l'ordre des clartés
sous son voile blanc derrière ses paupières fardées
ma ville gardait ses mystères
ne se consolait pas de sa beauté perdue
la porte de la mer n'ouvrait plus sur le large
négligeant nos plus belles légendes
nous vivions nos jours et nos nuits assis
autour du marbre d'une fontaine tarie

*

à seize ans j'avais le sourire grave
de qui rêve d'évasion
j'avais deux visages je vivais dans deux mondes
merveilleusement immobiles
des sphinx peuplaient mes jardins de sable
des oiseaux de feu traversaient mon ciel
fissures du silence dans le lent travail du jour
avec la mort pour horizon la mer nous retenait
ses cuisses de méduse ondulant sous nos doigts

*

nine years old dazzled I discovered a buried city
on the way back I laid my wings out to dry on the dunes
I counted stones before collecting them
I had two faces lived in two worlds

*

at eleven I already spoke to no one
and yet a language was being born in my mouth
I searched for the poem's secrets in silence
tried to place myself in the order of clarities
behind its white veil its painted eyelids
my city kept its secrets
unconsoled for its lost beauty
the door no longer opened out on the sea
neglecting our loveliest legends
we passed our days and nights seated
around a marble fountain that had gone dry

*

at sixteen I had the solemn smile
of someone dreaming of escape
I had two faces lived in two worlds
marvellously motionless
blind sphinxes lived in my gardens of sand
firebirds crossed my sky
fissures of silence in the day's slow labor
with death for a horizon the sea held us
its jellyfish thighs squirming beneath our fingers

*

nous vivions nos jours et nos nuits assis
autour du marbre d'une fontaine tarie
la porte de la mer n'ouvrait plus sur le large
des sphinx aveugles peuplaient mes jardins de sable
on y fit planter un palmier qui bientôt caressa les nuages
je restais à ses pieds les yeux au ciel
ma grand-mère apparut
c'est un signe dit-elle tu vas nous quitter
fit les recommandations d'usage
versa l'eau verte sous mon pas
pour que tu reviennes un jour dit-elle
déjà j'étais sur l'autre rive

*

à quarante ans toujours habitée par mes ombres
entre passé et avenir
je suis de mon enfance et donc de nul ailleurs
je me souviens d'une nuit jeune
vécue au rythme de la mer
il y avait entre le monde et moi
tant d'espace et si peu
l'enchantement la connivence
c'était avant la lente agonie de la planète
avant la fissure du masque
j'avais deux visages je vivais dans deux mondes
je rêvais des rides du désert
face à l'étreinte de l'horizon

*

we passed our days and nights seated
around a marble fountain that had gone dry
the door no longer opened out on the sea
blind sphinxes lived in my gardens of sand
a palm tree was planted there that soon caressed the clouds
I stayed at its foot my eyes on the sky
my grandmother appeared
it's a sign she said you'll leave us soon
gave the usual advice
spilled green water on my footsteps
so that you will return one day she said
I was already on the other shore

*

at forty still inhabited by shadows
between past and future
I come from my own childhood and not elsewhere
I remember a young night
lived to the sea's rhythm
between the world and me
there was so much space and so little
enchantment complicity
it was before the planet's slow dying
before the rift in the mask
I had two faces lived in two worlds
I dreamed of the desert's ridges
facing the horizon's blue embrace

*

je suis de mon enfance et donc de nul ailleurs
quelle vérité découvrir alors
que celle du soleil de chaque jour
celle d'une pluie de sable dans ma main ailée
la grande voix du monde
dans la trame unique
de la langue patiente qui me fut donnée

*

moi qui ne fais que partir qui ne fais que partir
chaque seuil franchi
j'avance vers ma mort vers le premier jour
ainsi se creuse notre solitude
comme on explore au fond d'un puits sans eau
pour l'ombre rien que pour l'ombre
et face à soi-même
ce lieu où gît un reflet de la lumière

*

loués soient les deux syllabes libres du soleil
l'archipel du silence où je trouve les mots
le voyage de seuil en seuil qui est le vrai voyage
loué soient celui qui s'égare
celui dont la parole est dans l'écart
loué soit le monde parce que tout existe
ailleurs que dans le poème et en lui

*

I come from my own childhood and not elsewhere
what truth then to discover
but that of each day's sun
of a rain of sand in my winged hand
the world's vast voice
in the thread's weft
of the patient tongue that was given me

*

I who am always returning always leaving
each threshold crossed
I move towards my death towards the first day
so our solitude digs in
as we'd explore the bottom of a dry well
for its shade only for its shade
face to face with ourselves
place where a glint of light is laid

*

praise be to the free syllable of sun
the archipelago of silence where I find words
the voyage from doorway to doorway which is the only voyage
praise be to the one who strays
whose word is set apart
praise be to the world for everything exists
elsewhere than in the poem and in it

*

toujours entre passé et avenir
j'ai voulu trouver celle qui devait être
je cherche désormais celle qui fut
je suis de mon enfance et donc de nul ailleurs
minuit de lumière alphabet du rien
mer blanche du soleil couchant
grande mer intérieure à l'ouest de nos rêves

*

always between past and future
I wanted to find the woman who should be
from now on I will look for the one who was
I come from my own childhood and not elsewhere
midnight of light alphabet of absence
white sea of the setting sun
great inland sea to the west of our dreams

je dis tu es ma blessure
et je dis vrai
le jour soudain s'assombrit
la mort halète dans mon sang
je me défais de ton regard
avant de renaître vierge à moi-même
à l'heure que tu choisis
ainsi distançant la nuit
tantôt je suis près
de la plus haute étoile
tantôt je marche obscure
sur une terre empruntée
et je ne sais plus ce qui est
préférable quand la nuit
alimente la mort
l'une créant l'espace de l'autre
que l'autre parcourt
pourtant le monde est beau

je dis tu es ma blessure
et je dis vrai et le rêve docile
te donne corps et visage
et je ne sais plus
dès que le jour est en vue
que ton regard m'invente et m'escorte
que je suis dessaisie
soudain à moi-même étrangère
affligée d'exil, mortelle,
ce qui est préférable –
m'interdire l'océan stérile du naufrage
tenter de comprendre ce qui demeure
inexplicable en nous
la tranquille absence des choses
la distance du monde nu dans sa lumière
ou continuer à croire
à la terre où je respire

you are my wound I say
and I speak the truth
all at once the day darkens
death gasps in my blood
I undo myself in your gaze
then am reborn virgin to myself
at the hour you choose
outdistancing the night
sometimes I am close
to the farthest star
sometimes walking shadowed
on borrowed ground
and I no longer know which is
preferable when night
nourishes death
one making a space for the other
that the other crosses
and yet the world is lovely

you are my wound I say
and I speak the truth and my tamed dream
gives you body and face
and I no longer know
when day comes into view
when your look invents and surrounds me
when I am suddenly
removed from, foreign to myself
afflicted with exile and mortal,
which is preferable –
to refuse the shipwreck's sterile ocean
and try to understand what remains
inexplicable in us
the tranquil absence of objects
the distance of a world naked in its light
or to continue believing
in the earth where I breathe

comme dans l'autre langue
se dérobe le secret des voyelles
signes invisibles que l'oeil recrée
j'inaugure la perte d'un visage

l'oeil est une étoile dans le ciel noir
une larme de lumière trace son sillon
dans la clarté qui fera le jour
la lame des corps tranchera l'espace

d'une rive antique nous portons la mémoire
se consume le flambeau du temps
l'être réfugié dans l'être cherche son ombre
langage parfait du silence

je m'applique à faire revivre
le passé dans mon oeil gauche
l'oeil droit que le soleil éclaire
s'invente un incertain futur

je ne conçois pas la terre sans le ciel
la lumière sans le sacrifice des ténèbres
l'eau sans la soif des pierres
le poème sans l'être le lieu sans la quête

je sais l'absolu du cercle et sa tension
la nuit et l'illumination l'ombre
et le seuil le feu et le symbole du feu
je suis mille je suis une

je commence et me recommence
dans l'infini des métamorphoses
dans le calendrier inépuisable du temps
j'accède au septième jour de toi

as in my other language
the secret vowels hide themselves
invisible signs an eye recaptures
I prepare for the loss of a face

the eye is a star in a black sky
a tear of light traces its furrow
in the brightening that will be day
bodies' blades slice into space

we bear the memory of an ancient shore
time's torch consumes itself
a being sheltered in itself seeks its shadow
silence's perfect speech

I apply myself to make the past
live again in my my left eye
the sunlit right eye
invents a dubious future

I don't imagine earth without sky
light without the sacrifice of darkness
water without the stones' thirst
an uninhabited poem a place without a quest

I know the circle's wholeness and its tension
night and illumination the shadow
and the threshold fire and the symbol of fire
I am a thousand I am one

I begin and I begin myself again
an infinity of metamorphoses
on time's inexhaustible calendar
I reach a seventh day of you

nous sommes les hôtes inconnus
dans la maison du monde
la mer la vague l'écueil
le navigateur découvrant
l'absence de balises

nous sommes l'oeil qui voit l'oeil
et la vision qui nous efface
nous sommes ce que nous regardons
au fond des yeux
et qui sait que nous sommes

nous sommes le nombre et l'unique
la chose et son contraire
la multiplication du visible
l'oeil ouvert sur l'invisible

nous sommes l'ombre de l'ombre
qui dans l'obscure clarté du rêve sommeille

nous sommes la trace sur le sable
nous sommes chaque lettre de l'alphabet

nous sommes l'oracle et l'hommage
le masque suspendu à l'arbre
le temple et l'objet offert
à la lumière morte du temple

nous sommes la question
qui n'appelle pas de réponse
nous sommes la question et la réponse
lorsqu'elles ne font qu'un

we are unknown guests
in the world's house
the sea the wave the reef
the navigator who discovers
there are no beacons

we are the eye which sees the eye
and the vision which erases us
we are the thing we stare at
deep in other eyes
which knows what we are

we are the number and the one
the object and its opposite
the multiplication of the visible
the eye open on the invisible

we are the shadow of the shadow
which sleeps in a dream's dark clarity

we are the line in the sand
we are each letter of the alphabet

we are oracle and homage
the mask hanging from the tree
the temple and what is offered up
in the temple's dead light

we are the question
which calls for no answer
we are the question and the answer
when they become one

nous sommes le cercle
qui se crée lui-même à l'infini
nous arpentons dans les deux sens
le calendrier des hommes
telle une échelle d'horizon
avant d'être invités à franchir
d'un bond le vide qui nous sépare
de notre naissance

oscillant entre ivresse et terreur
nous sommes ce que nous savons
et ce que nous ignorons
nous pleurons des larmes d'ambre

nous sommes le premier et le dernier mot
la strophe et le chant
et la bouche que nous voulons
accrocher à la face du silence

nous sommes la main insoumise
qui trace le signe
le vertige devant l'abîme
ouert par le poème

qu'une parole en nous hésite à se dire
nous atteignons le plus intime de la solitude

nous sommes le pas et la marche
le chemin et la voie
et l'ultime seuil que nous franchirons
nous sommes le lieu où finit le monde
celui où il commence

we are the circle
creating itself unto infinity
we go up and down the human calendar
in both directions
like a ladder against the horizon
until we are asked to breach
in one leap the gap which separates us
from our birth

wavering between intoxication and terror
we are what we know
and what we don't know
we cry for with amber tears

we are the first word and the last
the stanza and the song
and the mouth we'd like to
attach to the face of silence

we are the rebellious hand
which draws the sign
the vertigo facing the chasm
opened by the poem

if a word within us balks at pronouncing itself
we reach the most private of solitudes

we are the step and the course
the path and the way
and the last threshold which we will cross
we are the place where the world ends
and the place it begins

un instant le vent oublie
la pierre aimante de l'espace
l'ombre sans reflet
destinée à survivre au jour

nous parlons à voix basse
dans l'amitié des mots

l'âme est un arbre
et partout sur la terre
est le visage du poème
où les oiseaux viennent se poser

et la vie est un cheval blanc
dans le saut de l'abîme

et la tombe un seuil
loin des naissances terrestres

for an instant the wind forgets
the loving stone of space
the shadow with no reflection
destined to outlive the day

we speak softly
within the amity of words

the soul is a tree
and everywhere on earth
is the poem's face
where birds can land and perch

and life is a white horse
leaping the abyss

and the grave a doorway
far from earthly births

dans la poussière
toujours neuve
d'une parole habitée

nous avons tenté d'aller
comme le soleil
de l'autre côté de soi

nous avons lutté
pour conquérir notre être
trouver le Lieu
le meilleur des deux mondes

exprimer l'indicible
tel un arbre qui chante

il nous faut désormais oeuvrer
à conquérir le néant

in the always
new dust of
inhabited speech

we tried to go
like the sun
to the other side of the self

we have struggled
to conquer our being
to find the Place
the best of two worlds

to express the unsayable
like a singing tree

from now on we must work
to prevail over absence

nous fermons les yeux
je m'accorde au silence
le monde naît
une lame de ciel entre les yeux

nous fermons les yeux
une fois encore nos visages changent

nous fermons les yeux
une voix inconnue
appelle pour la troisième fois
l'écho témoigne

nous fermons les yeux
il faut qu'en nous les morts s'apaisent

we close our eyes
I attune myself to silence
the world is born
a blade of light between its eyes

we close our eyes
once again our faces change

we close our eyes
an unknown voice
calls for the third time
the echo bears witness

we close our eyes
the dead within us must calm down

je suis née d'un silence
entre la mer et l'olivier

le mystère d'une étoile errante
me protège de moi-même

je suis née d'un silence
entre la mer et l'olivier
du rythme des vagues
et de l'enfance de la lumière

les mots ont une face visible
qui en cache une autre

au carrefour du poème
quelques-uns résistent
m'exposent au risque de la parole

je suis née d'un silence
entre la mer et l'olivier
du rythme des vagues
et de l'enfance de la lumière
des noces de juillet d'une lune d'été
d'une évidence et d'une question

suspendue au souffle du monde
je m'inscris dans une douloureuse
errance le lieu où je demeure
est toujours une limite

je suis née d'un silence
entre la mer et l'olivier
du rythme des vagues

I was born of a silence
between the sea and the olive-tree

the mystery of an errant star
protects me from myself

I was born of a silence
between the sea and the olive-tree
of the rhythm of waves
and the childhood of light

words have a visible face
which hides another one

at the crossroads of the poem
some of them resist
expose me to the danger of speech

I was born of a silence
between the sea and the olive-tree
of the rhythm of waves
and the childhood of light
of July's wedding of a summer moon
of an obvious fact and of a question

hanging from the world's breath
I take my place in a sorrowful
wandering the place where I live
is always a border

I was born of a silence
between the sea and the olive-tree
of the rhythm of waves

et de l'enfance de la lumière
des noces de juillet d'une lune d'été
d'une évidence et d'une question
du vol solitaire de l'hirondelle
et d'un astre inconstant

ultime rendez-vous avec soi-même
la mort cratère bouche de feu
où abandonner ses dernières sandales

notre chemin part du soleil
pour rejoindre le soleil

and the childhood of light
of July's wedding of a summer moon
of an obvious fact and of a question
of a swallow's solitary flight
and of a fickle star

last meeting-place with yourself
death crater fiery mouth
where you leave your last pair of sandals

our path starts from the sun
to return to the sun

navires à la coque noire
flèche de l'éperon au ras de l'eau
rameurs soldats au bouclier rond
encens rêves prémonitoires
la lune repose entre les cornes
de la montagne bleue
la princesse a revêtu un manteau de pourpre
sur le large collier d'or le dieu
et la déesse chevauchant un lion
rythme des tympanons
ultime escale pour la princesse errante
ici fut jetée la pierre ici naîtra la ville nouvelle
ici les vierges de Kition
seront unies à leurs époux
après avoir délimité un territoire
c'est un temple que nous élèverons en premier
chevaux sans selles ni rênes des Numides
le nom de notre ville franchira les siècles
et cendres dispersées jamais
on ne retrouvera mon tombeau

black-hulled ships
arrow of the prow flush with the water
oarsmen, soldiers with round shields
incense premonitory dreams
the moon sleeps between the horns
of the blue mountain
the princess has put on a purple mantle
on her broad gold necklace the god
and the goddess astride a lion
strains of dulcimers
last port of call for the wandering princess
here the stone was thrown here the new city will be born
here the virgins of Kition
will be united with their spouses
after having marked out our borders
the first thing we build will be a temple
Numidian horses without saddles or bridles
the name of our city will outlast centuries
and ashes scattered forever
my grave will never be found

l'aube alertée se met en lumière
un soleil rond bientôt
fera chanter le ciel et la mer

debout sur la terre attentifs
aux faits du jour
le soleil devant nous
nous nous appartenons enfin

l'aube alertée se met en lumière

sur ces falaises s'arrête
le vol de l'épervier
ici se figent les doigts nouant
dénouant la plante pigmentée
qui donne la vie et la mort

ici naît le silence
quand l'être s'augmente d'un regard

ailleurs un poète quitte la cellule
du secteur deux cent trente-six
un bagne s'effondre dans les sables
un homme rejoint libre
le centre de la terre

l'été viendra peut-être
serons-nous encore là
debout sur la terre
le soleil derrière nous

alerted dawn lit up
a round sun soon
will make the sky and sea sing

standing on the earth attentive
to the day's occurrences
the sun before us
at last we belong to ourselves

alerted dawn lit up

the sparrow-hawk's flight
stops on these cliffs
here the fingers freeze which knot
and unknot the bright plant
which gives life and death

here that silence is born
when someone grows by a glance

elsewhere a poet leaves his cell
in sector two hundred and thirty-six
a prison sinks in the sand
a free man rejoins
the center of the earth

summer will come perhaps
we will still be there
standing on the earth
with the sun behind us

j'habite ici gare de Lyon au sous-sol
il dit tu me trouves quand tu reviens
et sous la cendre des néons soudain
le jour s'achève avant le jour

tes yeux m'ont arrêté il dit
meurt une flamme dans sa pupille
et le crépuscule soudain se noie
dans le verre vide de sa bouteille

comme moi tu parles plusieurs langues
il dit tu voyages beaucoup
supplice du voyageur immobile
et l'aube soudain meurt avant l'aube

je suis né à Jérusalem… il sourit
je suis né au Maroc, Salah, SDF
tu me trouves ici quand tu reviens
et la nuit soudain s'achève avant la nuit

trente-deux ans que je vis à Paris
il dit loin des prières de la mère
ténèbres des départs avortés
mer et désert chavirent dans sa mémoire

toi aussi tu viens d'ailleurs il dit
et les pierres gémissent d'absence
la terre s'arrête de tourner
jadis oui j'eus aussi un pays

I live here in the basement of the Gare de Lyon
he says you'll find me when you come back
and suddenly beneath the ash of neon lights
day was done before daybreak

your eyes stopped me he says
with a flame dying out in his own pupils
and dusk drowned itself suddenly
in the empty glass of his bottle

you speak several languages like me
he says you travel a lot
torture of the motionless traveler
and dawn died suddenly before dawn

I was born in Jerusalem... he smiles
I was born in Morocco, Salah, yes, homeless
you'll find me here when you come back
and night was over before nightfall

thirty-two years I've been living in Paris
he says far from my mother's prayers
darkness of failed departures
sun and sand churn in his memory

you come from somewhere else too he says
and the stones moan with absence
the earth stops turning
once yes once I also had a country

on voit à tes yeux que aimes ta vie
il dit… rien qu'un sourire solitaire
comme talisman pour l'âme
il reste sept portes à franchir

passé les sept portes et les mille et une épreuves
peut-être serons-nous délivrés
(si cela peut avoir un sens)
du sud de la folie   de la folie du sud

one can see in your eyes that you love your life
he says… only a solitary smile
as a talisman for the soul
there are seven doors left to pass through

the seven doors passed through and the thousand and one trials
perhaps we will be delivered
(if that makes any sense)
from the south of madness   the madness of the south

que le cri des hommes
se transforme
dans la nuit des arbres
dans l'exil et dans la rage
en géante flèche

oiseau solaire
proche et si lointain

let the human cry
be transformed
in the night of trees
in exile and in rage
into a giant arrow

solar bird
close and so far off

rosée sur la pierre du monde
j'aurai cherché un sens
sous le regard des astres
qui nous éclairent

forte de l'instinct de la nuit
j'aurai cherché un seuil le Lieu
la lumière   mes découvertes
autant de stèles dressées vers le ciel

j'aurai aimé cette terre
chéri joies et blessures
aimé ma solitude le silence
et le risque de la parole

j'aurai aimé l'amour resurgi soudain
comme un exil de plus
sacrifice
où se survivre à soi-même

j'aurai aimé
ce que je ne connaissais pas encore
et jusqu'à l'abîme
notre unique vérité

la lumière je l'aurai entrevue
avant de retrouver
infinis sous mes pas
les chemins de l'ombre

de quoi rêvais-je
dans ma nuit de femme
sinon de ce qui de nous
avait une chance de survivre

dew on the stone of the world
I'll have searched for a meaning
beneath the gaze of stars
which light our way

strong with the sense of the night
I'll have searched for a doorway, the Place
the light   my discoveries
so many stelae raised toward the sky

I will have loved this earth
cherished joys and wounds
loved my solitude silence
and the risk of speech

I will have loved love reappeared suddenly
like one more exile
sacrifice
through which you outlive yourself

I will have loved
that which I don't yet know
and till the last leap
our single truth

light I'll have glimpsed it
before finding, infinite,
beneath my feet
the paths of shadow

what did I dream about
in my woman's night
if not of what within us
might survive

ne tuez pas la lumière
la lumière de midi
celle de minuit
même si tout commence par la nuit

ne tuez pas la lumière
même réfugiée dans des morceaux d'étoiles
dans l'éclat d'une demi-lune
dans celui du regard

ne tuez pas la lumière
en nous
tel un vaisseau dans la nuit

don't kill the light
the light of noon
or of midnight
even if everything begins with night

don't kill the light
even sheltered in shards of stars
in the gleam of a half-moon
or of a look

don't kill the light
within us
like a ship in the night

même si je dois désapprendre le monde
pour découvrir de quels ailleurs nous venons
de quels ailleurs nous rêvons
vers quels ailleurs nous allons
et qui rêvent peut-être de nous
même si cent fois je perds
et retrouve le fil d'Ariane
je resterai debout dans la lumière

même si mes rêves ne me laissent pas dormir
que je ne trouve nulle part de repos
même si je sais que le temps
ne nous accordera qu'un soupir
sur les eaux profondes du désir
je remercierai la vie pour chaque joie
chaque souffrance chaque regard
chaque parole chaque silence partagés

même si notre voyage se poursuit
entre le jour et la nuit
sous un ciel qui nous demeure étranger
que le passé s'efface et se meurt malgré lui sous nos pas
même si les mots me laissent inconsolable
heureuse amoureuse désespérée
jusqu'à ce qu'advienne la grande nuit
je resterai debout dans la lumière

même l'esprit broyé
par les sombres prisons de la nuit
même la chair clouée
par les mains avides du monde
même oubliés la date et le lieu
exacts de ma naissance
je resterai debout dans la lumière

even if I must unlearn the world
to discover which elsewheres we come from
of what elsewheres we dream
towards which elsewheres we go
which perhaps dream of us
even if I lose Ariadne's thread
and find it again a hundred times
I will stand up in the light

even if my dreams don't let me sleep
if there's nowhere I find rest
even if I know that time
grants us only a sigh
across desire's deep waters
I will thank life for each joy
each sorrow each look
each word each silence shared

even if our journey continues
between day and night
beneath a sky which stays strange to us
if the past fades away and expires despite itself beneath our feet
even if words leave me inconsolable
joyful infatuated despairing
till the arrival of the great night
I will stand up in the light

even with my spirit crushed
by night's dark prisons
even with my flesh nailed down
by the world's grasping hands
even when the date and the place
of my birth are forgotten
I will stand up in the light

sève vénéneuse
en nos lignes de vie

quel fruit empoisonné
lentement mûrit en nous

je me vêtirai de ma mort
comme d'un soleil

poisoned sap
in our lifelines

what venomous fruit
ripens within us slowly

I will put on my death
like a sun

ce siècle sera celui de notre mort
je ne crains pas cela
qui se dresse devant moi
je vais mon chemin
s'arrêter serait mourir vraiment
un jour qui sait je reviendrai

ce siècle sera celui de notre mort
un instant nous avons fait
toi et moi le même rêve
une poignée d'étoiles entre les mains
quelle place lui accorder
parvenus au croisement des routes

ce siècle sera celui de notre mort
lumineuse obscure prends-moi
prends-moi même si l'amour
n'est pas l'unique réponse
sans mes prières sans cet amour
je ne verrais pas ainsi les choses de ce monde

ce siècle sera celui de notre mort
chaque regard chaque sourire chaque geste
chaque parole fut une offrande
malgré les tragédies passées
celles qui suivront
j'aurai oui j'aurai connu la joie

this will be the century of our death
I'm not afraid of what
rises before me
I go my way
to stop would be to die in earnest
one day who knows I'll come back

this will be the century of our death
for a moment you and I
had the same dream
a bundle of stars in our hands
what place could we find for it
arrived at the crossroads

this will be the century of our death
luminous shadowed take me
take me even if love
is not the only answer
without my prayers without this love
I would not see the things of this world as I do

this will be the century of our death
each look each smile each gesture
each word was an offering
despite past tragedies
and those to come
I will have yes I will have known joy

ce siècle sera celui de notre mort
dans la langue du silence
que je comprends mieux que celle que j'écris
la vie l'amour la mort prennent sens
toujours pour de nouveaux départs je serai prête

ce siècle sera celui de notre mort
comme toi j'appartiens
à la race de ceux qui toujours ont su
simplement regarder la terre
ceux qui toujours ont su
simplement regarder la terre

this will be the century of our death
in the language of silence
which I understand better than the one in which I write
life love death begin to make sense
I'll be ready always for new departures

this will be the century of our death
like you I belong
to the race of those who have always known
how to look at the earth simply
those who have always known
simply to look at the earth

SENTIER DE LUMIÈRE

> — *D'où es-tu venue?*
> — *De l'autre monde.*
> — *Et où vas-tu?*
> — *Vers l'autre monde.*
> ~Rabi'a al-'Adawiyya,
> *Chant de la recluse.*

j'ai dormi trois siècles sur un lit de rochers
j'ai vu des choses oubliées des hommes
j'ai mesuré la distance qui sépare le ciel de la terre
j'ai lu les lignes de la main j'ai rendu les oracles
une voix qui n'était pas ma voix a parlé par ma bouche
j'ai disparu dans une ville elle-même disparue
des cavaliers en armes ont envahi nos plaines
nous sommes restés dans l'attente d'autres barbares
la mer s'est retirée des portes de ma ville
je me suis concilié les fleuves de la terre
j'ai orné le jour du tatouage de mes rêves
mon visage a vu mon autre visage
je n'ai pas entendu la voix qui m'appelait
la main qui me cherchait ne m'a pas trouvée
je suis née plusieurs fois de chaque étoile
je suis morte autant de fois du soleil des jours
j'ai pris très tôt des bateaux pour nulle part
j'ai demandé une chambre dans la patrie des autres
je n'avais rien accompli avant nos adieux
j'ai habité le couchant le levant et l'espace du vent
j'étais cette étrangère qu'accompagnait le soir
deux fois étrangère entre nord et sud
j'ai gravé des oiseaux tristes sur des pierres grises
j'ai dessiné ces pierres et les ai habitées
j'ai construit des radeaux où il n'y avait pas d'océans
j'ai dressé des tentes où n'étaient nuls déserts

PATH OF LIGHT

> – *Where have you come from?*
> – *From the other world.*
> – *And where are you going?*
> – *Towards the other world.*
>   ~Rabi'a al-'Adawiyya,
>   *Song of the Hermit*

I slept for three centuries on a bed of stones
I saw things men had forgotten
I measured the distance that separates heaven from earth
I read the palm's lines I pronounced the augury
a voice not my own spoke from my mouth
I disappeared into a city that had disappeared
armed horsemen invaded our plains
there we stayed waiting for the next barbarians
the sea withdrew from the doors of my city
I gained the favor of the earth's rivers
I tattooed the day with my dreams
my face saw my other face
I did not hear the voice that was calling me
the hand that sought me did not find me
I was born many times from each star
I died as many times with each day's sun
I took the early boat headed for nowhere
I asked for a room in the country of others
I had accomplished nothing before our farewells
I lived in the setting sun the rising sun the wind's space
I was that foreign woman who came with evening
doubly foreign between north and south
I carved sad birds on gray stones
I drew those stones and inhabited them
I built rafts where there was no ocean
I pitched tents where there was no desert

des caravanes m'ont conduite vers un rêve d'orient
mes calligraphies ont voyagé sur le dos des nuages
je me suis souvenue de la neige des amandiers
j'ai suivi la route aérienne des oiseaux
jusqu'au mont de la lune aux duvets des naissances
j'ai appris et oublié toutes les langues de la terre
j'ai fait un grand feu de toutes les patries
j'ai bu quelques soirs au flacon de l'oubli
j'ai cherché mon étoile dans le lit des étoiles
j'ai gardé ton amour dans le creux de ma paume
j'ai tissé un tapis avec la laine du souvenir
j'ai déplié le monde sous l'arche des commencements
j'ai pansé les plaies du crépuscule
j'ai mis en gerbes mes saisons pour les offrir à la vie
j'ai compté les arbres qui me séparent de toi
nous étions deux sur cette terre nous voilà seuls
j'ai serré une ceinture de mots autour de ma taille
j'ai recouvert d'un linceul l'illusion des miroirs
j'ai cultivé le silence comme une plante rare
lueur après lueur j'ai déchiffré la nuit
la mort un temps m'a courtisée
j'ai cherché dans le soleil la direction du soleil
je me suis couchée dans ma tombe et me suis relevée
je me suis égarée puis retrouvée d'une genèse à l'autre
je t'ai attendu sans t'attendre
jusqu'à ce que tu deviennes poème
j'ai mêlé la chair à l'argile et à la lumière
j'ai mêlé le souffle à ce qui était déjà souffle
j'ai habité la maison chaude de ta voix
j'ai fait naître les souvenirs avant qu'ils n'aient vécu
j'ai caché mon amour sous les pudeurs de l'ombre
je me suis demandé comment le dire avant de le dire
et pourquoi je ne le disais pas
j'ai dit qu'il était temps que j'aille vers toi
j'ai rampé jusqu'à tes lèvres sur un lit de ronces

caravans brought me to a dream of the orient
my calligraphies traveled on cloud-back
I remembered the snow of almond trees
I followed birds' flight-paths
to the moon mountain to the eiderdown of birth
I learned and forgot all the languages on earth
I made a bonfire of all its homelands
some nights I drank from the flask of oblivion
I searched for my star in the bed of stars
I kept your love in the crease of my palm
I wove a carpet from the wool of memory
I unfolded the world under the arch of beginnings
I bandaged the wounds of twilight
I made bouquets of my seasons and offered them to life
I counted the trees that separate me from you
there were two of us on earth now we are alone
I pulled a belt of words tight around my waist
I covered the mirror's illusion with a shroud
I cultivated silence like a rare plant
glimmer by glimmer I deciphered the night
for a while death courted me
in the sun I sought the way to the sun
I lay down in my grave and rose again
I was lost and found between one genesis and the next
I waited for you without waiting
until you became a poem
I mixed flesh with clay and with light
I mixed breath with what was already breath
I lived in the warm house of your voice
I made memories come to birth before they had lived
I hid my love in shadows' modesty
I asked myself how to speak of it before speaking of it
and why I did not speak of it
I said that it was time to go towards you
I crawled to your lips across a bed of thorns

j'ai cru que ce qui nous unissait
était ce qui nous ressemblait
je me suis cherché en toi un pays une langue
en m'éloignant du rêve je m'en suis approchée
j'ai noirci des pages avec la nuit du poème
l'oiseau noir du silence les froissait une à une
j'ignore encore quelle langue me parle et m'absout
j'ai pris un sentier de lumière qui mène à l'horizon
mon pays : un bouquet d'adieux cueillis au fil du temps
j'ai déroulé ses rives comme une natte d'alpha
j'ai trouvé un nom pour ce qui reste de l'enfance
pour fleurir entre tes bras
j'ai jeté les oranges du souvenir dans un puits
j'ai dessiné mon amour à la craie sur une muraille d'eau
rien ne demeure dans la mémoire des hommes
je marchais en moi et loin de moi
une ombre parfois épousait mon ombre
à chaque départ je tranchais un lien
libérais l'oiseau de feu des cendres de la mémoire
je marchais en toi et loin de toi
je me suis alliée à l'alphabet du sable
aux ondulations de la vague
à la paix qui clôt tes paupières
mon chant sera à l'image de cette paix
j'ai reconnu l'aube à l'aube dans son regard
j'ai voulu le jour à l'image de ceux que j'aime
j'ai apprêté la nuit pour la moisson du rêve
j'ai courtisé le visible j'ai étreint l'invisible
j'ai tout lu de la terre dans le grand livre de la terre
j'ai témoigné de l'éphémère et de l'éternité de l'instant
je me suis attardée au seuil de chaque seuil
nos morts appelaient de l'autre rive
les lignes de leur monde sillonnaient nos mains
l'écho de leurs voix s'épuisait dans la distance
les suicides du sang étaient autant de pierres
dans les remparts du temps

I believed that what united us
was what resembled us
in you I sought a country a language
in drawing away from the dream I came closer to it
I darkened pages with the poem's night
the black bird of silence crumpled them one by one
I still don't know what language speaks me and absolves me
I followed a path of light that led to the horizon
my country : a bouquet of farewells gathered over time
I unrolled its shores like a mat of alpha
I found a name for what was left of childhood
to flower in your arms
I threw the oranges of memory into a well
I drew my love in chalk on a wall of water
nothing remains in human memory
I walked within myself and far from myself
sometimes a shadow embraced my shadow
severing a bond at each departure
freeing the firebird from memory's ashes
I walked within you and far from you
I allied myself with the alphabet of sand
with the wave's undulations
with the peace which lowers your eyelids
my song will be in the image of that peace
I recogized dawn from the dawn in its gaze
I wanted a day made in the image of those I love
I prepared the night for the harvest of dreams
I courted the visible embraced the invisible
I read about the earth in the great book of the earth
I bore witness to the ephemeral eternity of the instant
I lingered at the doorway of each doorway
our dead called from the other shore
the lines of their world furrowed the palms of our hands
the echo of their voices disappeared in the distance
the blood suicides were so many stones
on the ramparts of time

j'ai fait mes premiers pas dans le limon des fleuves
on m'a ensablée vive sous un amas de dunes
on a obstrué la caverne – que mon sommeil s'éternise
on a exilé mon corps à l'intérieur de mon corps
on a effacé mon nom de tous les registres
jusqu'aux épousailles des deux rives
j'ai porté en moi le vide comme la bouche d'un noyé
décembre a disparu derrière l'horizon
j'ai appelé – seul le silence était attentif
j'ai vu les siècles s'égarer jusqu'à nous
le grenadier refleurissait entre les stèles
ma ville changeait de maître comme de parure
ma terre : un nuage en marge du levant
pourquoi chercher un lieu quand nous sommes le lieu
mon ombre a gravi un long chemin jusqu'à moi
un jour je suis entrée dans la maison de la langue
j'ai niché deux oiseaux à la place du coeur
j'ai traversé le miroir du poème et il m'a traversée
je me suis fiée à l'éclair de la parole
j'ai déposé un amour insoumis dans le printemps des arbres
et délivré mes mains pour que s'envolent les colombes

I took my first steps in the river's silt
I was buried alive in sand under a mass of dunes
the cavern was blocked up to make my sleep eternal
my body was exiled to its own interior
my name was erased from all the registers
until the nuptials of the two riverbanks
I carried emptiness in me like a drowned man's mouth
December disappeared behind the horizon
I called out – only silence listened
I saw centuries stray until they reached us
the pomegranate tree flowered again between the stelae
my city changed its rulers like necklaces
my land : a cloud on the edge of the Levant
why seek a place when we are the place
my shadow climbed a long path to reach me
one day I entered the house of language
I nested two birds where the heart ought to be
I crossed the poem's mirror and it crossed me
I trusted the spark of the word
I placed a rebellious love in the trees' springtime
and freed my hands so that those doves could fly

Au présent du monde

je fus cette autre
dans l'étourdissement d'errances incertaines
du temps où vêtue d'eau pure et de soleils lisses
je grandissais encore sur une terre vraie
du temps où j'attendais tout de l'aube
de la nuit immortelle de l'enchantement du jour
de mon jumeau de sang et de mots
du temps où nos rencontres
étaient toujours une première fois
du temps où je devinais avant de comprendre
me diluais dans des jardins oubliés
du temps où la vie ne s'imaginait pas autre
où je revendiquais un lieu
dans la claire nudité du monde
où je connaissais les secrets de l'instant
où mon sang battait dans les veines du poème
où le silence précédait les mots
leur prêtant leur vision du temps où les mots
étaient des oiseaux sans racines
oiseaux de passion au ciel lourd d'attente
chutant comme dans un songe la fin du jour
du temps où je rêvais les yeux ouverts
où je m'obstinais entre le visible et l'invisible
où je cherchais la plus grande lumière
du temps où la mort n'avait pas été inventée
femme crépusculaire
puisant l'offrande des mots au puits du néant
j'eus tous les âges je n'ai plus rien
j'ai laissé une empreinte de corps
dans la nuit fêlée des villes
rien qu'une étape sans apaisement

I was that other
in the exhilaration of unsettled wandering
in a time when dressed with pure water and sleek suns
I was still growing on a real earth
in a time when I expected everything of dawn
of immortal night of day's enchantment
of my twin in blood and words
in a time when our encounters
were always the first
in a time when I guessed before I understood
diluted myself in forgotten gardens
in a time when life did not imagine itself other
when I claimed a spot
in the world's bright nakedness
when I knew the moment's secrets
when my blood beat in the poem's veins
when silence preceded words
lending them its vision in a time when words
were rootless birds
birds of passion in a sky heavy with waiting
dropping like a dream at dusk
in a time when I dreamed with my eyes open
when I persisted between the visible and the invisible
when I searched for the greatest light
in a time when death had not been invented
twilight woman
drawing a gift of words from the well of nothing
I was every age now I am none
I left a body's imprint
on the cracked night of cities
only a stopping-point with no relief

femme crépusculaire livrée aux failles
de l'ombre au masque derrière les visages

l'absence se mesure au bleu du silence
le temps me dessine de nouvelles frontières
sur le sel de la page
se projette l'ombre intérieure

il me faut un temps de rupture
que se poursuive l'errance

twilight woman given up to the flaws
in the shadow, to the masks behind faces

absence is measured by the blue of silence
time draws new frontiers for me
the inner shadow is cast
on the salt of the page

I need a time of rupture
to continue that journey

port de Durban de nuit
sur le bateau blanc
Chirikure mon ami
une Amstel dans chaque main
Vusi chante times are
good when we meet
welcome to South
Africa welcome
à Ilja je demande où suis-je
Gladman poète zoulou
nous conduit sur les routes
    de la poésie
je retrouve l'océan Indien
tambour à vif le soleil
se couche sur nos rêves
    je m'en vais
par les rues rectilignes
North Street East Street
West Street Durban blues
Smith Street Bottle Shop
l'alcool se vend derrière
des barreaux de fer
Durban blues
on vous sourit
on vous agresse
on vous tend la main
pour quelques rands
welcome to South
Africa welcome
les guerriers zoulous
guettent la nuit
à l'aube ils dansent
pour les touristes

Durban seaport at night
on the white boat
my friend Chirikure
with an Amstel in each hand
Vusi sings times are
good when we meet
welcome to South
Africa welcome
I ask Ilja where I am
the Zulu poet Gladman
drives us down roads
      of words
I find the Indian Ocean again
a peeled drum the sun
sets on our dreams
      I go off
down the rectilinear streets
North Street East Street
West Street Durban blues
Smith Street Bottle Shop
alcohol is sold behind
iron bars
Durban blues
you're smiled at
you're assaulted
someone puts out a hand
for a few rands
welcome to South
Africa welcome
the Zulu warriors
wait for nightfall
at dawn they dance
for the tourists

tambour à vif le soleil
triomphe de nos cauchemars
les mammas somnolent
derrière leurs étals
masques masques masques
de gros oiseaux gris
sondent les pelouses
les cocotiers lissent le ciel
    je m'en vais
par les rues rectilignes
Palmer Street Mile Street
Hunter Street Durban blues
Victoria Street Market
couteaux saris tripes
poissons tabac goyaves épices
masques masques masques
welcome to this mixed-up
country welcome
ce pays Antjie mon amie
ce pays est aussi
douloureusement tien
townships shacks shacks shacks
make this country
a livable place
Botha's Hills Thousand Hills
maisons rondes canne à sucre
vaches aux cornes solaires
petits singes bondissants
hameaux sans nom
les guerriers zoulous
ont rangé leurs lances
les seins des femmes
tressautent sous
l'abondance de perles
chante Vusi chante
ma mayibuye i Africa

a peeled drum the sun
overcomes our nightmares
the mammas snooze
behind their market stalls
masks masks masks
large gray birds
probe the lawns
coconut trees preen the sky
        I go off
down the rectilinear streets
Palmer Street Mile Street
Hunter Street Durban blues
Victoria Street Market
knives saris tripe
fish tobacco guavas spices
masks masks masks
welcome to this mixed-up
country welcome
this country Antjie my friend
this country is also
sorrowfully yours
townships shacks shacks shacks
make this country
a livable place
Botha's Hills Thousand Hills
round houses sugar cane
cows with solar horns
little leaping monkeys
nameless hamlets
the Zulu warriors
have put away their spears
women's breasts
bounce beneath
an abundance of pearls
sing Vusi sing
ma mayibuye i Afrika

welcome to KwaZulu-
Natal welcome
nous avons parlé
à l'ombre du marula
nous lisons poème après poème
Sheri-D mon amie oui
nous sommes ivres de vin
de mots en lisant je danse
je fais l'amour avec les mots
le silence se brise
en éclats de diamant
je suis un poème poème poème
qui meurt dans ma bouche
tu n'as rien vu à Durban
Durban blues Jo'burg blues
nous lisons poème après poème
Vusi chante bad are times
when parting keeps its way in
souviens-toi souviens-toi
de ce que tu as oublié
de voir à Durban

welcome to KwaZulu-
Natal welcome
we have talked
in the shade of the marula
we read poem after poem
Sheri-D my friend yes
we are drunk with wine
with words while I read I dance
I make love to the words
silence shatters
in diamond shards
I am a poem poem poem
which dies in my mouth
you haven't seen anything in Durban
Durban blues Jo'burg blues
we read poem after poem
Vusi sings bad are times
when parting keeps its way in
remember remember
what you forgot
to see in Durban

nous vivons dans un pays
ivre de violence et de guerre
Medellín sombrera dans la tristesse
dès votre départ nous resterons là
à attendre la lumière simplement
vous remercier d'être venus

…

merci d'être venus parmi nous
desplazados ayant fui nos villages
notre passé notre présent saccagés
quel avenir pour nos enfants ici à La Cruz
c'est notre âme qu'on nous a arrachée
là-bas avec notre terre

…

tirs sporadiques dans la montagne en face
tranquilla me dit une femme
sur le sentier du retour
les combats sont éloignés
sous les lentes spirales
des rapaces noirs
une bouteille de vin du Chili
circule de main en main

…

je ne sais rien de ce pays dis-tu
en Pennsylvanie on peut vivre tranquille
sans rien savoir du reste du monde
explique-moi dis-tu ta voix posée
telle une caresse laissée en suspens

…

we live in a country
drunk on war and violence
Medellín will sink into sadness
as soon as you've left we'll stay there
waiting for the light simply
to thank you for having come

...

thank you for coming to be here with us
desplazados who have fled our villages
our past our present laid waste
what future for our children here in La Cruz
it's our soul they've torn out
back there with our lands

...

sporadic gunfire from the mountain in front of us
tranquilla a woman says to me
on the path back
the fighting is far away
under the slow spirals
of black hawks
a bottle of Chilean wine
passes from hand to hand

...

I don't know anything about this country you say
you can live comfortably in Pennsylvania
and know nothing about the rest of the world
tell me about it you say your voice poised
like an interrupted caress

...

une bombe a explosé en pleine nuit
tout près de notre hôtel à Bogotá
cela m'a ouvert les yeux dis-tu
depuis j'ai cherché à comprendre
…
libertad hurle la foule debout
après la lecture d'un poème
dans l'amphithéâtre Carlos-Vieco
LIBERTAD

a bomb went off in the middle of the night
right next to our hotel in Bogotá
that opened my eyes you say
since then I've tried to understand
…
libertad cries the crowd standing as one
after a poem is read
in the Carlos-Vieco auditorium
LIBERTAD

au septième jour de ma naissance
je parlai le langage
du monde d'où je venais
témoignai de l'ombre
qui était l'ombre
d'un autre lumière
que personne ne voyait

au septième mois de ma naissance
ma bouche prit la forme du vide
je criai pour dire le vrai
et ce que le présent m'avait appris
du passé du futur
mais personne n'entendait

la septième année de ma naissance
je rêvai ce qui avait été
sur la page quadrillée du monde
je traçai lettre après lettre
pour me souvenir
de ce qu'il me faudrait oublier
et de ce qui déjà mourait en moi

on the seventh day of my birth
I spoke the language
of the world I'd come from
bore witness to a shadow
which was the shadow
of another light
which no one saw

in the seventh month of my birth
my mouth took the shape of the void
I cried to tell what was true
and that which the present had taught me
of the past of the future
but no one heard

the seventh year of my birth
I dreamed what had been
on the world's lined page
I traced letter after letter
to remind myself
of what I had to forget
and of what in me was already dying

j'eus dix ans le ciel en tête
j'empruntai ses ailes au soleil
pour voler vers ce lieu entre deux rives

j'élevai des tours de sable
qu'habitait l'ombre qui me servait de corps

corps mûri par un soleil d'extrême été
j'étais dans la pensée du vent
les tons de la lumière
composaient mon paysage

j'étais dans la couleur du jour
je grimaçais avec les pierres
où s'abritaient les scorpions
dans l'île les femmes portaient un masque
peut-être par pudeur

le ciel en tête je me faisais invisible
pour mieux voir frappais aux vitres
où se rassemblait le jour
en un hymne quotidien
je cherchais un sens à la forme –
au-delà le monde devait exister

j'eus vingt ans impatiente
d'aborder des continents neufs
je quittai la maison de mon père
livrai à la lumière ma liberté d'oiseau
entrai dans l'espace de l'obscur

je cherchai à ouvrir des portes invisibles
affirmai lire la matière même du silence
comme une langue natale
fis du passé un commencement
et du présent une double absence

I was ten years old head full of sky
I borrowed the sun's wings
to fly toward that spot between two shores

I built towers of sand
where that shadow lived which served as my body

body ripened by a sun of extreme summer
I was in the wind's thoughts
intonations of light
composed my landscape

in the color of day
I scowled with the stones
where scorpions sheltered
on the island, women went masked
perhaps out of modesty

sky in my head I would make myself invisible
to see better knocked at windowpanes
where the day gathered
in an ordinary hymn
I looked for meaning in form—
somewhere out there the world must exist

I was twenty years old impatient
to shore up at new continents
I left my father's house
gave my avian liberty up to the light
entered the space of darkness

I tried to open invisible doors
claimed to read the very stuff of silence
like a mother tongue
made a beginning of the past
and a double absence of the present

corps vivant plus que mort
je refusais que la nuit me sépare
du jour et le jour de la nuit

veilleur du rêve que le rêve invente
que cherchais-je lorsque j'ouvrais les yeux
sur les couleurs du monde
que jamais ne perd de vue le soleil

de la mémoire seconde des mots
naît l'émotion la plus réelle
j'habite cette musique
que je ne puis être seule à entendre

ombre qui suit ou précède son ombre
aux frontières entre rêve et réel
je demeure en marge de moi-même
dans l'espace et dans le temps

comment savoir si en ce lieu
de nulle part où se libère la voix
je suis venue de moi-même
ou s'il s'est imposé

body more alive than dead
I refused to let night separate me
from day or day from night

watcher of dreams whom a dream invented
what was I looking for when I opened my eyes
on the colors of the world
which the sun never lets out of its sight

from words' second memory
real feeling is born
I inhabit that music
which I can't be the only one to hear

shadow which follows or precedes its shadow
on the border between dream and real
I stay on my own margins
in space and time

how to know if in this nowhere
place where a voice sets itself free
I came of my own free will
or if it was imposed on me

enfant du soleil et de la terre
jusque dans l'ombre du soir que le jour tire à soi
je voyage dans la fibre étirée des nuages
dans la vague qui se joue de moi
à suivre la courbe enfiévrée des étoiles
qui s'éteignent dans l'encre de la mer
je m'endors sur la blancheur des dunes
à l'écoute du souffle des morts
dans les champs d'asphodèles

enfant du soleil et de la terre
je me penche sur le dernier puits de l'île
à l'affût de la danse secrète
des scorpions sous la pierre

bercée par le conte de ma grand-mère
qui ajoute un parfum dans le brasero du patio
je croque le fruit miellé du caroubier
la nuit venue je me penche sur l'écho
que renvoie le fond de la citerne interdite

enfant du soleil et de la terre
j'accompagne mon père dans les jardins de son père
où veillent les oliviers centenaires
je grimpe au mûrier blanc la poulie grince
va-et-vient du chameau à la mémoire longue

enfant du soleil et de la terre
je récite les versets sacrés
seule fille parmi les garçons
assis sur la natte de l'école coranique

enfant du soleil et de la terre
je voyage dans les arabesques des murs
dans le chant pur du rossignol à la cime du citronnier
dans les phrases mystérieuses des livres
dans le rayonnement gris des yeux de ma mère

child of the sun and the earth
until day pulls evening's shadow toward itself
I roam through the thinned threads of clouds
through the wave which plays tricks on me
following the fevered curve of stars
which burn out in the sea's ink
I go to sleep on the dunes' whiteness
listening to the dead breathing
in their fields of asphodel

child of the sun and the earth
I lean over the last well on the island
to spy on the secret dance
of scorpions under the stone

rocked by my grandmother's story
as she puts incense in the courtyard brazier
I bite into the honeyed carob-fruit
when night comes I bend over the echo
that the forbidden cistern sends back to me

child of the sun and the earth
I go with my father to his father's gardens
where hundred-year-old olive trees keep watch
I climb the white mulberry-tree, the pulley creaks
the long-memoried camel comes and goes

child of the sun and the earth
I recite the sacred verses
the only girl among the boys
sitting on the woven mat of the Coranic school

child of the sun and the earth
I travel in the walls' arabesques
in the nightingale's pure song at the lemon-tree's crown
in books' mysterious sentences
in the glow of my mother's grey eyes

je suis enfant et libre
d'habiter d'éternels dimanches
soleil posé sur l'horizon
dans la clarté de toute chose
la terre contemple ses saisons
je n'ai lieu ni demeure
la vie est partout et nulle part

dans la citerne du patio l'aïeule puise
l'eau pour le basilic et la menthe
pile le sel et les épices
livre son combat quotidien au réel
la brise gonfle les rayures du rideau
la lampe brille encore
je joue de l'autre côté des images

dans les jardins de mon père
les arbres portent des fruits anciens
chuchotent dans la langue des oiseaux
l'eau du puits chante dans les sillons
sous mon pas naissent des chemins de sable
je suis dans l'innocence du jour
pur commencement sans avant ni après

d'une maisonnette construite tel un bateau
je me laisse couler dans l'émotion bleue
un ballet d'hippocampes frôle
les étoiles tombées du ciel
des oursins fleurissent les rochers
des algues scintillent à mon poignet
seul vit l'instant dans ce que je contemple

144

I am a child and free
to live in perpetual Sunday
sun perched on the horizon
in each thing's clarity
earth contemplates its seasons
I have no place or dwelling
life is everywhere and nowhere

from the courtyard cistern the grandmother draws
water for the mint and basil
grinds the salt and spices
wages her daily battle with the real world
the breeze swells out stripes on the curtains
the lamp still glows
I play beyond the pictures

in my father's gardens
the trees bear ancient fruit
whisper in the birds' language
well-water sings in the furrows
beneath my steps sand-paths are born
I inhabit the day's innocence
pure beginning with no before or after

from a little house built like a boat
I let myself flow into blue emotion
a sea-horse ballet brushes
against fallen stars
sea-urchins blossom on the rocks
seaweed glitters on my wrist
only the moment lives in what I gaze at

je suis enfant et libre
je n'ai lieu ni demeure
vaste est l'horizon quand le monde
tout entier est poème
il fait grand jour sur la terre
la nuit n'est pas encore créée
j'ai pied dans tous les temps

I am a child and free
I have no place or dwelling
how vast the sky is when the whole
world is a poem
it's broad daylight on earth
night has not yet been created
I have a foothold in all of time

tu te doutes de la patience
de cette terre fauve
quand ses yeux s'absentent
pour s'ouvrir sur le bleu
qui colore son sens

comme toi comme le poème
cette terre est née
du regard qui l'a rêvée

la vie est une traversée
entre deux rives

analogie des marges
lent mouvement vers l'inachevé
chant d'innocence et de mémoire

scribe dans la nuit de la langue
quand la nuit parle la langue du néant
tu es sur cette terre
pour cultiver ton âme
apprivoiser ce qu'il y a d'humain
dans l'angoisse
habiter la parole de la parole
et conserver la promesse du poème

you can guess the patience
of this lion-colored earth
when its eyes absent themselves
to open on the blue
which colors its sense

like you like the poem
this earth is born
of the look that dreamed it

life is a crossing
between two shores

analogy of margins
slow movement toward the unfinished
song of innocence and memory

scribe in the night of language
when night speaks the language of noughts
you are on this earth
to grow your soul
tame what's human
in dread
inhabit the word's word
and keep the poem's promise

L'Absence l'inachevé

contrée incertaine pétrifiée endeuillée
feu fer sang barbelés
Djibouti médite au bord de la mer Rouge
les boutres pourrissent dans l'anse du port
Rimbaud assis pensif sur un pupitre d'écolier
n'a plus d'encre pour sa plume
ni de papier pour un poème

kilomètre 12 village de tôle de réfugiés
bidons d'eau rouillant le long des pistes
cônes jumeaux des volcans jaillis du sang de la mer
tels seins de femme pointant vers le soleil
arbustes en triangle soutenant l'étendue du ciel
pasteur nomade debout sur un rocher scrutant l'infini
la tombe d'un saint homme se signale par un chiffon vert
à l'extrémité d'une hampe plantée dans un amas de pierres
un cercle de pierres brunes dessine une mosquée
champs de lave noire où grouillent les serpents
sourire édenté de la faille en travers de la piste
lac Assal oeil de sel grand ouvert sur un autre ciel
montagnes bleues mauves violettes du rêve éthiopique
traversées de caravanes chargées de sueur et de sel

Maskali rêve d'île d'oiseaux de coraux de sables blancs
escale et refuge d'Henri de Monfreid
idiomes des paysages et des hommes
inscrits en signes éphémères
chaque terre est notre terre et une autre terre
chaussé de sandales de cuir le dernier aventurier
hésite devant l'étal entre une mâchoire de requin
des bracelets qui ont fait le voyage sur l'océan Indien
et une Bible de nomade en langue amharique

uncertain land petrified mourning
fire iron blood barbed wire
Djibouti meditates on the Red Sea shore
dhows rot in the cove of the port
Rimbaud seated pensive at a school desk
has no more ink for his pen
no paper for a poem

kilomètre 12 sheet metal refugee village
big water containers rusting alongside the path
the volcanoes' twin cones burst from the blood of the sea
like a woman's breasts pointing toward the sun
triangular bushes holding up the stretch of sky
nomad pastor standing on a rock scanning infinity
a holy man's tomb is marked with a green cloth
tied to a pole thrust in a pile of rocks
a brown rock circle marks out a mosque
fields of black lava swarming with snakes
toothless smile of the rift across the trail
Lake Assal eye of salt open wide on another sky
blue mauve purple mountains of the Ethiopian dream
passage of caravans loaded with sweat and salt

Maskali dream of an island of birds of coral of white sands
port of call and refuge of Henri de Monfreid
dialects of landscapes and men
inscribed in ephemeral signs
this earth is our earth and another earth
wearing leather sandals the last adventurer
hesitates at the market stall between a shark's jaw
bracelets that crossed the Indian ocean
and a nomad's Bible in Amharic

depuis les tourelles du château de Heidelberg
les vignobles s'étendent à perte de vue
méandres paresseux du fleuve miroitant au soleil
je m'essouffle à escalader le chemin des Philosophes
monastère fortifié aujourd'hui en ruine au coeur de la forêt
théâtre à l'antique pour la liturgie hitlérienne
avant la retraite aux flambeaux
c'est Pâques dans les rues pavées de la vénérable cité
où le Philippin José Rizal vécut un temps et étudia

from the turrets of Heidelberg Castle
vineyards stretch as far as the eye can see
indolent curves of the river shimmer in sunlight
I'm out of breath from climbing the Philosophers' Trail
a walled and moated monastery in the forest's heart a ruin today
Greek-style theater for Hitlerian liturgy
before the torchlit recessional
it's Easter in the old town's cobblestoned streets
where the Filipino José Rizal lived for a while and studied

oiseaux de mauvais augure
au-dessus de Gorée la noire
roches basaltiques cernant l'île aux esclaves
cellules sombres chaînes de fer porte du non-retour
au loin le continent Dakar le port plus loin encore
au-delà de la mer et du désert ton pays dit Hawad
et plus loin encore les îles de la déportation

baobabs cercueils surgis de la terre rouge du Sahel
vers la voûte chauffée à blanc d'un ciel sans nuées
offrande sanglante d'un dieu vivant à la majesté de la nuit
une lune géante monte lentement dans un rêve de ciel
tempête et embruns sur l'immensité du lac Débo
villages de terre s'abandonnant aux sables des berges
des chevaux blancs et libres caracolent dans le vent
le fleuve trace son cours sur un parchemin hors du temps
sur la rive se dresse le tombeau de la vierge
sacrifiée pour que naisse et perdure
la ville de terre aux ruelles de poussière
soupirs dans l'air du soir ou est-ce le fleuve qui pleure ?
labyrinthe du palais qui cisèle ses pierres roses
croissants de lune noirs des pirogues sur les eaux
les poissons séchés débordent des paniers tressés
des enfants tracent à l'ombre d'un mur
la parole sacrée sur leur tablette de bois
et pour l'éternelle faim des hommes verdissent les carrés
de blé et de riz à la lisière des dunes blondes

sur la lumière de Tombouctou
le vent jette un voile de sable
tombeaux des saints ensablés dans la pierraille
le gardien de la mosquée m'offre une fleur
de cotonnier l'imam une poignée de sable

birds of ill omen
above black Gorée
basalt boulders encircling the island of slaves
dark cells iron chains the door of no return
the continent far off the port of Dakar still farther
beyond the sea and the desert is your country says Hawad
and farther still the islands of deportation

baobabs coffins thrusting up from the red earth of Sahel
towards the white-hot vault of a cloudless sky
bloody offering of a living god to the night's majesty
a giant moon rises slowly through a dream of sky
storm and seaspray on enormous Lake Débo
earthen villages giving themselves over to the sand of its shores
free white horses prancing in the wind
the river traces its course on timeless parchment
on the riverbank rises the tomb of the virgin
sacrificed for the birth and survival
of the earthen town with its lanes of dust
sighs rise in the evening air or is it the river weeping?
the labyrinth of the palace that chisels its pink stones
black crescent moon pirogues on the waters
dried fish overflowing the braided baskets
in the shadow of a wall children trace
the sacred words on their wooden slates
and for man's eternal hunger squares of wheat
and rice turn green alongside the blonde dunes

the wind throws a veil of sand
across the light of Timbuktoo
saints' tombs with sand covering the loose stones
the guardian of the mosque gives me a cotton-
flower the imam a handful of sand

hommes femmes enfants remodèlent
maisons et temples de terre
avant qu'ils ne retournent à la terre
puis la foule se prosterne dans le sable grège

au soir repas et poèmes sous un ciel orphelin d'étoiles
quand résonnent les tambours caravanes des douleurs
j'ai jeté l'ancre au creux d'une dune
amarrée hors du temps
cette terre est notre terre et une autre terre
idiomes des paysages et des hommes
inscrits en signes éphémères

men women children are reshaping
houses and temples of earth
before they return to the earth
then the crowd prostrates itself in beige sand

in the evening a meal and poems beneath a sky orphaned of
    stars
when the drums sound—caravans of grief
I dropped anchor in the crevice of a dune
moored outside time
this earth is our earth and another earth
dialects of landscapes and men
inscribed in ephemeral signs

sourcils étonnés des ponts d'Amsterdam
sur le reflet gris des eaux
bateaux ivres des brumes de novembre
dans le dédale du vent je sillonne un rêve de pierre
et d'eau traverse une place un tableau un parc
une arche sur le parapet un héron immaculé rêve
de ses cousins d'Afrique et des Caraïbes
exposées regard absent derrière les vitrines
de longues femmes brunes venues d'au-delà des mers
tu dis certains quartiers ne sont pas sûrs ici
loin de la ville face à la fenêtre de la pièce où tu écris
la prairie le bosquet aux arbres couleur d'or
le ciel a l'éclat des plus belles perles
chaque terre est notre terre et une autre terre
idiome des paysages et des hommes
inscrits en signes éphémères
nous buvons verre après verre pour réveiller
les souvenirs d'un autre automne

Amsterdam's bridges raised eyebrows
above the water's gray reflections
drunken boats of November fog
in the wind's labyrinth I cut through a dream of stone
and water cross a square a painting a park
an archway on the parapet a pristine heron dreams
of his African and Caribbean cousins
staring absent on display behind shop windows
tall brown women arrived from beyond the seas
you say some neighborhoods aren't safe here
far from the city facing the window of the room where you write
the prairie the grove of golden trees
the pearly brilliance of the sky
this earth is our earth and another earth
dialects of landscapes and men
inscribed in ephemeral signs
we drink glass after glass to reawaken
memories of another autumn

anse du port de Durban
où dansent les lueurs de la ville
silence des arbres dans l'éternel été silence de l'océan
d'où chaque matin se hisse un jour nouveau
silence sur les pelouses où paissent des oiseaux gris
silence du poète bras tailladé par la lame rouillée
parodies de masques tournés vers le silence du ciel
citadins ivres de bière dès que tombe le rideau
de la nuit chacun barricadé dans son silence
parce que trop de mots demeurent imprononçables
ces mots que hurlera Sandile sur scène et ailleurs
comme la lame rouillée hurla dans le bras du poète

baraques à la périphérie villages abandonnés de l'intérieur
femmes en robes fleuries dans l'attente de l'improbable
petits singes curieux sur le bord des routes
halte sous l'enivrant marula l'arbre à liqueur
soudain je parle d'un voyage au coeur d'un autre désert

cove of Durban's port
where the lights of the city are dancing
the trees' silence within eternal summer the ocean's silence
from which a new day is hoisted each morning
silence on the lawns where gray birds graze
silence of the poet his arm slashed by a rusty blade
parodies of masks turned toward the silent sky
citizens drunk on beer as soon as night's curtain
falls each one barricaded in silence
because too many words remain unsayable
those words that Sandile shrieked on stage and elsewhere
the way the rusty blade shrieked through the poet's arm

shacks on the outskirts abandoned villages within
women in flowered dresses waiting for the improbable
curious little monkeys by the roadsides
a stop beneath the heady marula the liquor tree
all at once I speak of a voyage to the heart of another desert

feux du soleil couchant sur la Baie de Manille
marins en attente d'un navire prostituées bars néons
sur le trottoir un marin américain compte des billets
la jeune femme le remercie d'un bras d'honneur
le peso philippin continue de s'effondrer
dans la citadelle je mets mes pas dans ceux
de José Rizal de la chapelle au lieu de son exécution
jeepneys déments dans les rues défoncées
la queue du typhon me noie sous ses trombes
quand la terre tremble les tours de verre se lézardent
messe en tagalog dans l'église de Quiapo
à mon tour je caresse le pied de la statue
du Nazaréen noir ployé sous sa croix
dehors sur les étals herbes écorces poudres amulettes
peaux de serpent chapelets boules de verre
devant Solidaridad Bookshop un homme âgé
portant un sac de journaux récupérés lit penché
sur la vitrine la une de l'Asia Wall Street Journal puis
celle du Time : comment en finir avec la pauvreté
au matin Tessie nomme pour moi les fleurs
nouvellement écloses aux arbres de son jardin
idiomes des paysages et des hommes
inscrits en signes éphémères
chaque terre est notre terre et une autre terre

direction le centre et le nord de Luzon
de petits hérons sont plantés vigies blanches
dans le vert incomparable des rizières
le paysan ilokano qui nous accueille à Bangkalog
a lu tous les livres que Frankie a écrits et d'autres
les petites villes se succèdent
la place l'église les maisons le marché couvert
où flotte l'odeur tenace du coprah
Frankie prend la pose devant son ancienne école
et la statue d'un paysan avec son buffle

flames of sunset on Manila Bay
sailors waiting for a ship prostitutes neon bars
on the sidewalk an American Marine counts his bills
the young woman thanks him with a fuck-you finger
the Filipino peso keeps diving
in the citadel I place my soles
in the citadel I place my soles in José Rizal's footsteps
from the chapel to the place where he was shot
demented jeepneys in the ripped-up streets
the typhoon's tail drowns me in its torrents
when the earth trembles the glass towers splinter
mass in Tagalog in Quiapo church
I take my turn stroking the foot of the statue
of the black Nazarene bent beneath his cross
outside on market stalls herbs tree-bark powders amulets
snakeskins rosaries glass balls
in front of Solidaridad Bookshop an old man
carrying a bag of collected newspapers reads bent
towards the window the headlines of the *Asia Wall Street Journal*
then *Time*'s: how to put an end to poverty
in the morning Tessie tells me the names
of the newly-blooming flowers on the trees in her garden
dialects of landscapes and men
inscribed in ephemeral signs
this earth is our earth and another earth

towards the center and to the north of Luzon
little herons stand white lookouts
in the incomparable green of the rice-paddies
the Ilokano farmer who greets us at Bangkalog
has read all Frankie's books and others too
one little town comes after another
the square the church the houses the covered market
where the odor of copra persists
Frankie poses in front of his old school
and the statue of a peasant with his buffalo

165

à Banawe les rizières en terrasses
sont un miroir brisé où se mire le ciel
sources éboulements troncs arrachés rocher
géant au détour de la route de montagne
nous sommes en plein ciel nous traversons les nuages
nous pourrions rouler au fond du précipice
finir écrasés comme punaises par un de ces rocs
ou rester bloqués plusieurs jours
plaisante à peine Frankie

dans l'église de Laoag (lumière)
un mariage est célébré en anglais
la fanfare de la ville suivie de majorettes
accompagne un mort jusqu'à sa dernière demeure
souvenir de la fillette d'Olongapo
dans les bras une géante poupée blonde
la très vieille femme sur le golfe de Lingayen
qui propose crabes et crevettes dans un van immense
se souvient peut-être des bombardements américains
silhouettes menues accroupies dans les champs
mausolée sombre à Sarrat où dans le sarcophage
de verre repose qui sait le corps de Marcos
plantations de caféiers dans le paysage embrumé
en route vers Tagaytay sur un muret :
Responsibility is enthusiasm
puis jaillit le volcan Taal du miroir paisible de son lac

baie de Subic au bord de la mer de Chine
je fais un bouquet de branches de corail mort
arbres tropicaux bananiers petits singes furieux
en bordure de la jungle dans le ciel crépusculaire
tournoie un peuple d'oiseaux noirs
idiomes des paysages et des hommes
inscrits en signes éphémères
chaque terre est notre terre et une autre terre

at Banawe terraced rice-paddies
are a broken mirror reflecting the face of the sky
water-sources piles of earth uprooted tree-trunks giant
rock at the detour on the mountain road
we are up in the sky we cross clouds
we could roll to the foot of the precipice
be flattened like fleas by one of these rocks
or be trapped there for a few days
Frankie quips barely joking

in the church at Laoag (light)
a marriage is celebrated in English
the village brass band followed by majorettes
accompany a dead man to his last resting place
I remember the little girl at Olongapo
with a huge blonde doll in her arms
the very old woman on the gulf of Lingayen
selling crabs and shrimps from an enormous van
may remember the American bombardments
slight silhouettes bent over in the fields
dark mausoleum at Sarrat where in a sarcophagus
of glass rests who knows the body of Marcos
coffee plantations glimpsed through fog
on the way to Tagaytay on a low wall:
Responsibility is enthusiasm
then the Taal volcano surges up from its lake's peaceful mirror

Subic Bay on the shore of the China Sea
I make a bouquet of coral branches
tropical foliage banana trees furious little monkeys
on the edge of the jungle in the sunset sky
circles a populace of black birds
dialogues of landscapes and men
inscribed in ephemeral signs
this earth is our earth and another earth

long trajet depuis La Guaira jusqu'à Caracas
maisonnettes roses jaunes bleues des ranchitos
menacés par la boue à chaque saison des pluies
volumes de l'Encyclopédie de Diderot et d'Alembert
dorés sur tranche à la Bibliothèque nationale
pieusement conservées aussi
des lettres autographes de Simon Bolivar
dans le jardin du musée d'antiques roches noires
sculptées par les Indiens arawaks
un homme gratte son cuatro serré sur son coeur
de retour de l'émission marathon du Presidente
Conceiçao nous commande caipirinha
sur caipirinha et m'entretient de ses amours
juste avant le chant du poète indien
en hommage aux esprits de la montagne
nous arrivons au théâtre Tereza Carreño
pour jouer notre partition

aéroport de Maiquetia l'avion minuscule d'Aeropostal
survole îlots montagnes anses bleues
plongé dans The Last Bow de Conan Doyle
Ernesto Cardenal n'a pas quitté son béret
ni le Che imprimé sur le tee-shirt du maire poète

vieilles maisons hollandaises de Barcelona
dignidad progreso slogans électoraux sur les murs
le public déborde du théâtre à l'italienne
plainte d'une contrebasse dans la nuit illuminée
Ernesto reçoit la plus haute distinction d'Anzoategui
rochers couverts d'iguanes face aux îles bleutées
flèche dressée dans la moiteur caraïbe
un long héron blanc porteur de quel message secret

all the long way from La Guaira to Caracas
little pink yellow blue houses ranchitos
menaced by mud each rainy season
gilt-edged volumes of Diderot and d'Alembert's Encyclopedia
at the National Library
where Simon Bolivar's handwritten letters
are also reverently preserved
in the museum garden ancient black rocks
sculpted by the Arawak Indians
a man plucks the strings of the cuatro clutched to his heart
just back from the Presidente's marathon broadcast
Conceiçao orders us caipirinha
after caipirinha and catches me up on her love affairs
just before the Indian poet's song
in homage to the mountain spirits
we arrive at the Teatro Tereza Carreño
to play our piece

Maiquetia airport the tiny Aeropostal plane
flies above islets mountains blue coves
immersed in Conan Doyle's *The Last Bow*
Ernesto Cardenal hasn't removed his beret
or the Che printed on the poet-mayor's T-shirt

old Dutch houses from Barcelona
dignidad progreso electoral slogans on the walls
the crowd overflows the Italian style theater
moan of a double bass in the glittering night
Ernesto receives the highest honor of Anzoategui
rocks teem with iguanas facing bluish islands
arrow drawn in the Caribbean damp
a tall white heron bearer of what secret message

169

ondulations bleues à l'horizon de Santa Ana de Coro
des oiseaux migrateurs survolent l'arbre du voyageur
Coro ville du vent et des dunes chantantes
Joel dessine le mot POESÍA sur le sable
que faisons-nous d'autre sinon écrire sur le sable
me poursuit le désert
idiomes des paysages et des hommes
inscrits en signes éphémères
chaque terre est notre terre et une autre terre

blue undulations on the horizon at Santa Ana de Coro
migrating birds fly over the traveller's tree
Coro city of wind and singing dunes
Joel writes the word POESÍA in the sand
what else do we do but write in the sand
the desert insists to me
dialects of landcapes and men
inscribed in ephemeral signs
this earth is our earth and another earth

oublions ce que le temps achève en nous
et parlons de commencements

je voudrais revoir la mer que ton regard
s'arrête un instant sur mes eaux

là-bas les peuples vivent proches de leurs dieux
à chaque seuil franchi font un voeu

là-bas juillet est une saison à plein temps
les chandelles des morts veillent sur les amoureux

à y songer je m'emplis d'émotion
ouvre ma porte au lointain
me fais oiseau pour renouveler mon chant
et pleure sur chaque blessure de cette terre

let's forget what time finishes in us
and speak of beginnings

I'd like to see the sea again and have your gaze
pause for an instant on my waters

people live close to their gods there
make a vow as they cross each threshold

July is a full-time season there
the candles of the dead watch over courting couples

to think of it fills me with feeling
I open my door to distance
become a bird to renew my song
and weep for each wound in this earth

retour après retour
je revenais dans la douleur
vers un homme qui alors
se souvenait de moi

l'histoire pour trouver sa fin
a multiplié la distance
jusqu'à l'apaisement
un beau jour d'avril
me délivrant de ce poids d'amour

aussi je puis me lasser
que tu reparaisses toi
qui jurais depuis ton jardin déserté
de ne jamais disparaître
parmi les brumes
de ton pays sans arbres

returning and returning
I would come back in sorrow
toward a man who
remembered me then

to find its end the story
multiplied distance
until its resolution
on a fine April day
relieving me of this burden of love

and I could become weary
of your reappearances you
who swore in your deserted garden
never to disappear
into the fog
of your treeless country

printemps
où j'entrai soudain
avec une âme neuve
telle une gerbe d'abandon

un temps nous aurons bu
aux mêmes sources
le monde allié rayonnant
avait le regard fiévreux
de ce qui commence
je parvenais au silence
le désir dans le sang

voici venus les nuits sans rêves
où les lunes se consument
l'effondrement des jours
dans l'indifférence du soleil

ton nom est désormais blessure
tu as pris un chemin pour me perdre
exil définitif

je parcours mes horizons intérieurs
s'enlisent les souvenirs les ombres
les désirs les joies les vertiges
coeur déserté
où s'inscrit la fêlure des saisons

je ne sais plus vers qui je vais

a spring
I entered suddenly
with a soul new
as a bouquet of abandonment

once we would have drunk
from the same sources
the conjoined shining world
had the feverish look
of something beginning
I achieved silence
with yearning in my blood

now here are dreamless nights
whose moons consume themselves
days collapse
in the sun's indifference

from now on your name is a wound
you took a path to lose me
definitive exile

I prowl my inner horizons
memories shadows are sinking there
desires joys vertigos
deserted heart
where the rift in the seasons inscribes itself

I no longer know toward whom I go

souvenirs d'enfances anciennes
le conte s'enracine dans l'éclat du jour
ses branches creusent
le terreau de la nuit

les colombes sont des femmes
qui se sont perdues dans le ciel
dit le conte

ma grand-mère est une colombe
qui s'est perdue dans le ciel du temps

son silence est une longue nuit

et si un jour j'étais moi aussi une colombe
perdue dans le ciel du temps
me reconnaîtrais-tu?

memories of past childhoods
the tale takes root in daybreak
its branches dig into
the soil of night

the doves are women
who got lost in the sky
says the tale

my grandmother is a dove
who got lost in the sky of time

her silence is a long night

and if one day I too were a dove
lost in the sky of time
would you recognize me?

le silence avait rendez-vous
avec son destin de silence
dans le jardin de l'exil
derrière ta maison

j'ai fait un feu de mots
me suis couverte
de leurs cendres
blessure inépuisable

entre les midis et les minuits
effacés des horloges
il y a l'espace du tout
l'espace du rien

à peine avons-nous franchi
le seuil dans un sens
que nous le franchissons
dans l'autre

silence had an appointment
with its silent destiny
in the garden of exile
behind your house

I made a fire from words
covered myself
with their ashes
self-renewing wound

between the clock's erased
noons and midnights
is the gap of everything
and nothing

the moment we've barely crossed
the threshold in one direction
when we cross it again
in the other

chaque jour le soleil égorge son spectre
et se lève dans son sang

tout commencement dessine un cercle
la mémoire mène à la mer des commencements
la jetée est de pierre l'arbre d'exil
j'aspire à l'horizon

sur un fil de lumière
je vais vers ce lieu qui est toi
et ce qui fut advient

une étoile danse sur le ciel de mon front
l'oiseau en nous renaît de la rive de l'âme
ta parole est tienne mienne est ma parole

tu rejoins le lieu que je suis
et le poème continue de s'écrire

nous sommes la pierre et le chant
le silence intense l'ombre le rêve et la distance
de nous-même à nous-même

je vois ton visage et l'ombre sur ton visage
comme le poème la souffrance se partage
nous compatissons à l'arbre aux saisons
trop brèves et à l'exil des saisons
aux sourires et aux déchirements de la terre
aux malheurs des hommes aux prières des femmes

à nos voeux l'instant prend sa forme éblouie
le temps s'efface tel un paysage
nous vivons les deux moitiés de nos vies
comme un voyage qui se souviendrait peut-être

daily the sun slits its own ghost's throat
and rises in blood

each beginning draws a circle
memory leads to the sea of beginnings
the pier is made of stone the tree of exile
I aspire to the horizon

on a thread of light
I move towards the place that is you
and what had been happens

a star dances on my forehead's sky
the bird within us is reborn from the soul's shore
your word is yours mine is my word

you return to the place that I am
and the poem continues to write itself

we are the stone and the song
the deep silence the shadow the dream and the distance
from ourselves to ourselves

I see your face and the shadow on your face
like the poem suffering is shared
we share the grief of the tree of the too-brief
seasons and of the exile from seasons
of the smiles and the rifts of the earth
of men's misfortune of women's prayers

as we would wish the instant takes its dazzled form
time blurs over like a landscape
we live the two halves of our lives
like a journey that will perhaps remember

du nom des îles des oiseaux des ports
du sillage blanc des navires des villes des êtres
du cycle des arrivées et des départs

et nous tombons amoureux de la nuit
parce que chaque nuit célèbre les noces du rêve
et nous tombons amoureux du jour
parce que la vie commence avec chaque jour

the names of islands birds ports
of the white wake of boats cities beings
of the cycle of arrivals and departures

and we fall in love with night
because each night celebrates a dream's wedding
and we fall in love with day
because life begins with each day

je m'absente du lieu
le retrouve en toi
le proche surgit du lointain
tranquille évidence

je suis auprès de toi
souffrant d'un excès de vie
d'un excès de mort

calligraphie de ton sang
sur la pâleur du drap

tu rêves et délires
dans ta langue
— elle suscite le lieu
mais quel est le lieu

nous ne pouvons bannir le mot coeur
il ne cesse de battre
dans chacun de nos silences

les feux du jour font des ténèbres
leurs confidentes
qu'attendent nos ombres
postées sous les arcades

je suis l'autre dans tes yeux
je suis l'autre dans les yeux de chacun

I leave the place
find it again in you
what's near springs from what's distant
tranquil evidence

I am beside you
as you suffer from too much life
too much death

calligraphy of your blood
on the sheet's pallor

you dream and hallucinate
in your language
—it creates the place
but which place?

we cannot banish the word heart
it doesn't stop beating
in each of our silences

the day's flames make darknesses
their confidants
our shadows wait for them
stationed beneath the archways

in your eyes I am the other
in all eyes I am the other

toi qui n'es plus dans le présent du monde
mais dans un excès de nuit aux seuils introuvables
je te façonne à ton image et caresse tes eaux

nous nous regardons nous éloigner
et le rêve ombre la nuit jamais indifférente
pour resurgir de tout son poids d'aérienne souffrance

je te garde multiple
dans le creuset des haleines fécondes
dans les corolles butineuses du silence
au coeur de la parole en fragments d'aurores
ressuscitées dans le frisson du jour prodigue

simplement je me repose de ton rêve
des soleils dans les yeux
il en va de certains rêves
comme d'un grand bonheur d'une grande douleur

à ton silence quand la voix manque
au rêve que tu portes dans ta nuit

il faut nourrir la flamme et protéger la lampe

you who are no longer in the world's present tense
but in an excess of night with hidden doorways
I create you in your own image caress your waters

we watch ourselves draw apart
and the dream shadows a never-indifferent night
then reemerges in all its weight of aerial pain

I keep you multiple
in the crucible of fecund breath
in the pollen-gathering corollas of silence
at the heart of words made of shattered dawns
brought back to life in a prodigal day's shivering

more simply I'm taking a rest from your dream
with suns in my eyes
it's that way with certain dreams
as with great happiness or great sorrow

for your silence when there is no voice
for the dream that you bear in your night

the flame must be fed the lamp protected

chaque jour se renouvelle
dans l'absolu de la lumière

comme les yeux qui habitent les têtes
de grands soleils s'aveuglent
aux paysages du monde

miroirs épineux
jeux d'ombre et de lumière

libéré enfin de ton corps
où t'en es-tu allé

each day renews itself
in absolute light

like eyes alive in our heads
huge suns blind themselves
on the world's landscapes

thorny mirrors
games of light and shadow

freed at last of your body
where have you gone

ce rien qui advenait
à l'instant où tu disparaissais
ce rien qui advenait
à l'instant où je regardais où
tu ne regardais pas
à l'instant où je regardais où
tu n'étais plus
où je n'étais pas
ce rien qui advenait
à l'instant

pas même une parole
pour dire ce rien

that nothing that was happening
at the moment you were disappearing
that nothing that was happening
at the moment I was looking where
you weren't looking
at the moment I was looking where
you no longer were
where I no longer was
that nothing that was happening
that moment

not even a word
to say that nothing

JUSQU'AUX LENDEMAINS DE LA VIE

désormais les mères dorment seules
parmi les portraits des morts
elles seules savent où ils s'en sont allés
et comment le long travail du mourir
déjà les séparait du vivant

les mères désormais seules errent
parmi les tombes des défunts
récitant le long des avenues de la mort
des prières en des langues inconnues
égrenant le lourd chapelet du temps écoulé

elles ne comptent plus le temps
aux nuits qui tombent sur la terre
ni aux matins qui se lèvent sur le monde
à tous elles demandent où commencent
où finissent les territoires de la mort

les mères découvrent la solitude
le monde circonscrit à un carré de terre dure
elles refont le même rêve qui entrebâille les ténèbres
conversent avec le vide des miroirs
redisent la même prière où se meurt la lumière du jour

désormais entre les draps défaits du temps
les mères célèbrent leurs noces solitaires
dans le silence profond des maisons
des horloges sans aiguilles
rythment le passage des heures

THE MOTHERS

from now on the mothers will sleep alone
among the portraits of the dead
only the mothers know where they've gone
and how the long labour of dying
had distanced them already from the living

alone from now on the mothers wander
among the graves of the departed
reciting down those avenues of death
prayers in unknown languages
telling the heavy beads of dispersed time

they no longer measure time
by nights that fall across the earth
nor by mornings rising on the world
they ask everyone where the territories
of death begin and where they end

the mothers discover solitude
the world shrunk to a square of hardened earth
they keep having the same dream that cracks darkness open
converse with the emptiness of mirrors
repeat the same prayer in which daylight is dying

from now on in the rumpled sheets of time
the mothers celebrate solitary weddings
in the deep silence of their houses
clocks without hands
mark the passage of the hours

désormais la nuit a des yeux
qui traquent l'insomnie des mères
en elles habitent les deux anges qui demain
nous demanderont des comptes quand notre tour
viendra d'approcher les portes du ciel

le fil du chapelet rompu
les mères versent l'eau de leurs larmes
dans la coupelle des tombes
elles surveillent le vol des oiseaux
les messages des morts entre leurs ailes

notre seconde demeure se dresse
dans l'avenue de la mort disent les mères
pourquoi avons-nous donné la vie
pour jusqu'à notre dernier souffle
la disputer à l'ombre

des nôtres nous ne voyons qu'os blanchis
nos mains souillées de la terre des cimetières
nous plantons arbres et arbustes que leurs branches
soient le toit de leur nouvelle demeure
si seulement nous avions su disent les mères

nous relisons les lettres des défunts
et imaginons des réponses neuves
tout s'éclaire lorsqu'il est trop tard
nous n'avons plus assez du fil des regrets
pour assembler les morceaux de notre nuit

nos mains tremblent disent encore les mères
à contempler de trop profondes ténèbres
nos yeux ne voient presque plus la lumière
les soleils ont déserté nos jardins et les nuages
en de longs haillons gris pendent aux arbres

from now on night will have eyes
tracking the mothers' sleeplessness
two angels inhabit them who one day
will ask for our accounts when our turn
comes to approach the doors of heaven

with the rosary's thread broken
the mothers pour the water of their tears
into the graves' crucible
they pay attention to the flight of birds
messages from the dead between their wings

our second home is built
in the avenue of death say the mothers
why have we given life
just to struggle for it with the shadow
until our own last breath

all we see of our kin is bleached bones
hands soiled with graveyard earth
we plant trees and bushes so those branches
will be the roof of their new dwelling
if only we had known say the mothers

we reread letters the dead once sent
and imagine different answers
everything becomes clear once it is too late
there is not enough thread of regret
left to string the shards of our night

our hands tremble the mothers say again
from looking into too much darkness
our eyes can barely see light
the suns have deserted our gardens
long rags of cloud hang from the trees

tous nous dansons accrochés tels des pantins
au bout de la corde du temps
nos gestes sont la réplique
de gestes anciens et personne désormais
n'entend notre parole expropriée

que n'aurions-nous fait pour ceux que nous aimons
ôtant les échardes du bouquet épineux de la vie
puis une à une les roses se sont flétries
désormais depuis le cadre d'une fenêtre
nous contemplons les noces de la mer avec l'horizon

notre vie une lueur vacillante environnée d'ombre
peu à peu nous nous défaisons de nos vertèbres
chaque jour courbées davantage
par le poids dérisoire de la mémoire
et par l'attente de notre propre fin

we all dance suspended like puppets
with time holding the strings
our movements replicate
ancient gestures and from now on no one
will hear our expropriated speech

what wouldn't we have done for our loved ones
plucked the splinters from life's thorny bouquet
then one by one the roses wilted
from now on through a windowframe
we will watch the sea marry the horizon

our life a glimmer that flickers on shadow
slowly we divest ourselves of our backbones
hunched over further each day
with the inconsequential weight of memory
and with waiting for our own end

AMINA SAÏD is the author of fourteen collections of poems, most recently *Les Saisons d'Aden*, published in 2011 by les Éditions al-Manar, the second of a trilogy beginning with *Tombeau pour sept frères*, published in 2008 with illustrations by Hassan Massoudy. Her six titles published with les Éditions de la Différence include *L'Absence l'inachevé* (2009), *Au présent du monde* (2006), and *La Douleur des seuils* (2002). She is also the author of two collections of retold Tunisian folk tales, *Le Secret* (Criterion, 1994) and *Demi-coq et compagnie* (L'Harmattan, 1997). She received the Jean Malrieu Prize in 1989 for *Feu d'oiseaux* and in 1994 the Charles Vildrac Prize. Her third book, *Sables funambules*, was translated into Spanish by Myriam Montoya in 2006, and other work has been translated into Arabic, German, Turkish, and Italian in journals or at the worldwide literary festivals in which she often participates. Born in Tunisia in 1953, Saïd has lived in Paris since 1979.

MARILYN HACKER is the author of twelve books of poems, including *Names* (Norton, 2009), *Essays on Departure* (Carcanet Press, UK, 2006) *Desesperanto* (Norton, 2003), and an essay collection, *Unauthorized Voices* (University of Michigan Press, 2010). Her ten volumes of translations from the French include Marie Etienne's *King of a Hundred Horsemen* (Farrar Strauss and Giroux, 2008), which received the 2007 Robert Fagles Translation Prize and the 2009 American PEN Award for Poetry in Translation; Hédi Kaddour's *Treason* (Yale University Press, 2010), and Vénus Khoury-Ghata's *Nettles* (Graywolf Press, 2008). For her own work, she is a past recipient of the Lenore Marshall Award, the Poets' Prize, the National Book Award, two Lambda Literary Awards, and the American PEN Voelcker Award for poetry in 2010. She is a Chancellor of the Academy of American Poets.

TITLES FROM BLACK WIDOW PRESS

TRANSLATION SERIES

Approximate Man and Other Writings
by Tristan Tzara. Translated and edited
by Mary Ann Caws.

Art Poétique by Guillevic.
Translated by Maureen Smith.

The Big Game
by Benjamin Péret. Translated with an
introduction by Marilyn Kallet.

Capital of Pain by Paul Eluard.
Translated by Mary Ann Caws, Patricia
Terry, and Nancy Kline.

Chanson Dada: Selected Poems by Tristan
Tzara. Translated with an introduction and
essay by Lee Harwood.

*Essential Poems and Writings of Joyce Mansour:
A Bilingual Anthology*
Translated with an introduction by
Serge Gavronsky.

Essential Poems and Prose of Jules Laforgue
Translated and edited by Patricia Terry.

*Essential Poems and Writings of
Robert Desnos: A Bilingual Anthology*
Edited with an introduction and essay
by Mary Ann Caws.

EyeSeas (Les Ziaux) by Raymond Queneau.
Translated with an introduction by Daniela
Hurezanu and Stephen Kessler.

Furor and Mystery & Other Writings
by René Char. Edited and translated by
Mary Ann Caws and Nancy Kline.

The Inventor of Love & Other Writings
by Gherasim Luca. Translated by Julian
and Laura Semilian. Introduction by
Andrei Codrescu. Essay by Petre Răileanu.

La Fontaine's Bawdy
by Jean de la Fontaine. Translated with an
introduction by Norman R. Shapiro.

Last Love Poems of Paul Eluard
Translated with an introduction by
Marilyn Kallet.

Love, Poetry (L'amour la poésie)
by Paul Eluard. Translated with an essay
by Stuart Kendall.

Poems of André Breton: A Bilingual Anthology
Translated with essays by Jean-Pierre
Cauvin and Mary Ann Caws.

Poems of A.O. Barnabooth by Valéry Larbaud.
Translated by Ron Padgett and Bill Zavatsky.

Preversities: A Jacques Prévert Sampler
Translated and edited by Norman R. Shapiro.

The Sea and Other Poems by Guillevic.
Translated by Patricia Terry. Introduction
by Monique Chefdor.

To Speak, to Tell You?
Poems by Sabine Sicaud. Translated by
Norman R. Shapiro. Introduction and notes
by Odile Ayral-Clause.

forthcoming translations

Essential Poems and Writings of Pierre Reverdy
Edited by Mary Ann Caws. Translated by
Mary Ann Caws, Patricia Terry, Ron Padgett,
and John Ashberry.

A Life of Poems, Poems of a Life by Anna de
Noailles. Translated by Norman R. Shapiro.
Introduction by Catherine Perry.

MODERN POETRY SERIES

An Alchemist with One Eye on Fire
by Clayton Eshleman

Anticline by Clayton Eshleman

Archaic Design by Clayton Eshleman

Backscatter: New and Selected Poems
by John Olson

The Caveat Onus by Dave Brinks.
The complete cycle, four volumes in one.

Concealments and Caprichos
by Jerome Rothenberg

Crusader-Woman by Ruxandra Cesereanu.
Translated by Adam J. Sorkin. Introduction
by Andrei Codrescu.

Curdled Skulls: Poems of Bernard Bador
Translated by the author with Clayton
Eshleman.

Endure: Poems by Bei Dao
Translated by Clayton Eshleman and
Lucas Klein

Fire Exit by Robert Kelly

Forgiven Submarine
by Ruxandra Cesereanu and Andrei
Codrescu

The Grindstone of Rapport:
A Clayton Eshleman Reader
Forty years of poetry, prose, and translations.

Packing Light: New and Selected Poems
by Marilyn Kallet

The Present Tense of the World:
Poems 2000–2009
by Amina Saïd. Translated with an
introduction by Marilyn Hacker.

Signal from Draco: New and Selected Poems
by Mebane Robertson

forthcoming
modern poetry titles

City Without People: The Katrina Poems
by Niyi Osundare

Exile is My Trade: A Habib Tengour Reader
Translated by Pierre Joris.

from stone this running by Heller Levinson

Larynx Galaxy by John Olson

Memory Wing by Bill Lavender

LITERARY THEORY / BIOGRAPHY SERIES

Revolution of the Mind:
The Life of André Breton
by Mark Polizzotti. Revised
and augmented edition.

WWW.BLACKWIDOWPRESS.COM